CHARRED & SMOKED

CHARRED & SMOKED

More Than 75 Bold Recipes and Cooking Techniques for the Home Cook

CHEF DEREK BUGGE & JAMES O. FRAIOLI

PHOTOGRAPHY BY MARY DEE MATEO

Skyhorse Publishing

Visit our website at www.skyhorsepublishing.com.

10 9 8 7 6 5 4 3 2 1

Library of Congress Cataloging-in-Publication Data is available on file.

Cover design by Jenny Zamenek
Cover photo credit iStock

Print ISBN: 978-1-5107-3157-8
Ebook ISBN: 978-1-5107-3158-5

Printed in China

CONTENTS

INTRODUCTION

Charring and smoking food have likely been around since the dawn of cavemen, when meats and vegetables were cooked over an open flame in smoky caves using primitive tools. The first smoker didn't appear on the market until the late 1930s, revealing that incorporating smoke into foods wasn't just something that occurred unintentionally when cooking with fire. The commercial smoker represented a culinary breakthrough to create more complexity in food, offering new aromas and tastes while making the food more interesting to eat. Today, the art of charring and smoking has progressed even further thanks to innovative technology, advanced kitchen appliances, and more efficient tools and equipment for the job. Across the globe, home cooks and professional chefs continue dedicating countless hours to testing the limits of what they can char and smoke using different fuels, temperatures, durations, methods, and products. In the end, the basic steps of charring and smoking remain relatively the same as they were thousands of years ago when that first piece of food was cooked over hot coals.

It's worth noting that the method of charring and smoking, along with searing, burning—all those techniques for achieving mouthwatering dishes with crispy textures and deep robust flavors—are not limited to the world of barbecue. Many in the culinary industry who've mastered the exciting art of food and fire are now referring to this savory result as the "fifth taste" after sweet, salty, sour, and bitter. In fact, fire and smoke are showing up far beyond barbecue on today's menus across the country, which is why you're not going to find brisket, ribs, or pulled pork in this book. Instead, you're going to be introduced to and taught how to prepare innovative and delicious meals using everyday food throughout the pages of *Charred & Smoked: More Than 75 Bold Recipes and Cooking Techniques for the Home Cook.*

From the comfort of your own kitchen or backyard grill, you'll learn through the easy and informative pages ahead that infusing everyday food with char and smoke is not a fad or accident but a culinary technique that requires persistence and practice to achieve that exciting new world of flavor.

I'm a culinary school graduate who's worked the grill at notable taquerias, bars, restaurants, oyster houses, champagne parlors, and country clubs throughout the Pacific Northwest, drawing inspiration from my Latin roots. Time spent in the kitchen with my parents and family has taught me how properly burning, charring, and smoking ordinary food increases the flavor profile of many dishes and allows me to entertain friends and guests with new menu options that draws them in and whets their appetite. Incidentally, charred food has deep roots in many cuisines, from Caribbean and Mexican to Turkish and American.

Today, I continue to develop, prepare, and serve up savory charred and smoked-infused dishes at home and at Ascend Prime Steak & Sushi, soon to be one of the hottest new restaurants in Bellevue, Washington.

Because studies have shown that deeply charring meats can produce chemicals that increase the risk of cancer if eaten on a regular basis, not everything in *Charred & Smoked* is burnt to a crisp. In fact, the majority of recipes only suggest a brief char or smoke. And because studies also show that most carcinogens are found in charred meats, most of the recipes in *Charred & Smoked* lean toward a bevy of garden-fresh vegetables, fruits, and wild sustainable seafood.

If you're ready to improve on a classic or would like to try something new, open the pages of *Charred & Smoked* and begin your culinary journey. For example, next time try grilling your tomatoes before tossing them on a salad or burger or charring your scallions before adding them to a marinade or sauce. Your dishes will elevate you to the next level thanks to the irresistible sweet and smoky flavors that emerge. You'll also learn how to purposely burn chilies and spices, which is the secret to enhancing dishes with even bolder flavor and aroma. You'll discover what foods stand up well to a little char, and I will introduce you to many of these delicacies through recipes like Charred Broccolini with Burnt Lime Dressing and Caramelized Beet Bites with Whipped Chévre &

Toasted Pistachios. The same holds true with fruits. Natural sugars lead to caramelization, providing home cooks with the right amount of bitterness to counter all that sweetness from, say, a strawberry or peach. And what about those used lemon and lime peels left behind on the cutting board? That's throwing away free flavor. I will teach you how to make your next salad dressing or side dish much more exciting by incorporating charred citrus. Charring and smoking also takes various proteins like poultry, pork, and seafood to the next level, as you'll see through such celebrated recipes as Smoked Pork Chop with Burnt Orange Glaze and Caramelized Scallops with Toasted Barley Risotto & Nettle Pesto. There's also recipe chapters on rubs, seasonings, dressings, marinades, sauces, creative cocktails, and even desserts using fire and smoke, as well as a run-through of the cooking methods used throughout the book and some essential equipment and tools you should have on hand.

So what are you waiting for? Open the book and begin your gastronomic voyage into the exciting world of charring and smoking everyday food for richer and more robust flavor!

COOKING METHODS IN THIS BOOK

The following cooking methods used throughout the pages ahead provide one essential function: transferring heat needed to cook your food. Take a moment and familiarize yourself with all of these methods so you can apply one or more techniques the next time you find yourself charring or smoking a particular food.

BAKING

Baking is often performed in the oven, using a long dry heat. However, when it comes to charring and smoking food, baking in hot ashes or with hot stones helps impregnate such food with much more earthy,

smoky flavors—something an oven cannot provide. Because not everyone has hot ashes or hot stones at their disposal, the oven and its simplicity will be used primarily throughout this book when it comes to baking.

BLANCHING AND SHOCKING

Blanching is a culinary technique home cooks should know. It's how you get your charred or boiled vegetables to look bright and vibrant yet perfectly cooked. To blanch vegetables, batches of vegetables are quickly added to a large pot of boiling water over high heat (salt, which is optional, may be added) for

2 to 5 minutes, depending on the vegetable. Another option is to char the vegetables in a skillet with a little olive oil over high heat. Then remove the vegetables and immediately plunge them into an ice-water bath (comprising a suitable-sized bowl filled with ice and water) to stop the cooking process. This is known as "shocking" the vegetables. Once cool, remove the vegetables and drain. Just before serving, add the vegetables to a pot of warm (not boiling) water to reheat, then remove and drain again before serving.

BLISTERING

Blistering is a simple technique, used especially when working with vegetables. To blister a vegetable, such as peppers, begin by adding some hot oil to a cast-iron skillet or other heavy skillet over medium-high heat. The key here is getting the pan scorching hot. Once to temperature, add the peppers. They will begin to sizzle and cook while their outer skins get nicely charred. Turn the peppers occasionally for even charring, but don't shake the pan. Shaking lowers the heat level. Some vegetables, like peppers, will begin to burst as the liquid inside them boils and ruptures the outer wall. This is okay. Continue to blister the peppers, and remove once there's a nice even char on the outer skins.

BRAISING

Unlike baking, which relies on long, dry heat, braising uses moist heat. Often used when cooking tough cuts of meat like a rump roast, moist heat helps break down the connective tissues of beef,

resulting in meat that is soft and tender. Braising is best achieved in the oven, which uses indirect heat, after the meat has been properly browned or charred on the stove over high heat. The charred beef is then transferred to the oven with plenty of braising liquid (broth, stock, or wine), which should barely cover the meat. At a temperature setting of 250°F to 300°F, meat should braise for about 1 hour per pound. The result will be beef that is tender and succulent.

BRINING

Brining is the process of submerging food such as beef and poultry into a brine solution, typically overnight. Brines usually consist of water and salt,

although sugar and a variety of aromatics are often added. The meat then absorbs this solution, thereby decreasing any moisture loss during the cooking process, resulting in a juicier and flavorful dish. When smoking meat or seafood, it's also best to brine the meat or fish beforehand, which adds more tenderness and flavor to the finished product.

CARAMELIZING

Caramelizing is the process of cooking the food's natural sugars so they brown and become sweet and nutty with a hint of bitterness. Fruits such as apples, bananas, peaches, along with onions, carrots, and other fruits and vegetables benefit from being

caramelized. Sugar, itself, can also be caramelized (page 42). Caramelization is often performed in a hot pan with some olive oil or butter, or a combination thereof. You add foods, such as sliced onions, to the pan and cook over a period of time, while stirring occasionally, until the onions break down and achieve a rich caramelized color.

CHARRING

Charring is the process of naturally and purposely blackening (or burning) the exterior or outer crust of meat, fruits, and vegetables by grilling, roasting, broiling, or caramelizing to achieve a more robust, smoky flavor along with a crispy texture. There's really no limit as to what food can be charred. The important rule to understand when it comes to charring is learning heat control. You will want to start hot, char the exterior, then finish the cooking process by finishing in an oven, similar to braising. A great way to char is to place food over the hottest part of a fire or grill, then remove the food as soon as it's blackened.

DEEP-FRYING

Like its name suggests, deep-frying is performed when food is submerged and cooked in hot oil, resulting in a crisp, golden-brown exterior while the inside of the food is moist and tender. Deep-frying begins with a sturdy, heavy-bottomed pot or, ideally, a home deep-fryer. The most important rule when it comes to deep-frying is to exercise extreme caution when working with hot oil. Handy tools to make your deep-frying experience more efficient include a fine mesh skimmer, a wire draining rack, and a deep fat/candy thermometer. Always make sure to drain your fried food on a draining rack or absorbent paper towels. Also avoid introducing salt or spices into the hot oil, as this will greatly decrease the oil's frying life.

EMULSIFYING

Emulsifying is a technique used to combine two or more liquids together that normally wouldn't bond with one another. Good examples are oil and vinegar or oil and water. By whisking these two liquids into one homogenous state, the liquids will bond, but only for a short period of time, as the two liquids will soon separate and return to their natural state. To keep the liquids from separating, slowly whisk while adding the emulsifiers, which are your other ingredients, depending on what you're making. These emulsifying ingredients, such as mustard or eggs, whisked into the liquids will keep your emulsification stable, resulting in a smooth, creamy aioli, dressing, or sauce that doesn't separate. This is the art of emulsifying.

GRILLING ▶ ▶ ▶

When it comes to grilling, there are several primary methods for achieving high heat to char and cook your food: wood burning, charcoal (hardwood lump or briquettes), and gas (natural or propane). Which method is better? There's definitely pros and cons

to each. Ideally, it's best to have both a wood fire or charcoal grill and a gas grill when it comes to outdoor cooking. With wood fire and charcoal, you get real fire, resulting in higher heat and a more authentic smoky flavor, especially if using hardwood lump charcoal and incorporating presoaked wood chips. Although preheating the wood fire or charcoal grill can take some time, along with the cleanup because you're working with real ashes, the results are often well worth the time spent. With gas grills, it's all about convenience with little cleanup. However, you don't often get that real smoke flavor, which is why adding wood chips is often recommended. Regardless of which method of grilling you prefer, always keep the grill clean. Oiling your grill before cooking also helps to prevent sticking. If using charcoal, try to avoid lighter fluid, as it often expels a "chemical" smell and taste.

PREHEATING

Preheating the Outdoor Grill

As discussed in the Grilling method (page 8), there are many options when it comes to selecting an outdoor grill, whether it be wood burning, charcoal, or gas. In fact, no two grills are alike, yet the foundation is the same. It is important to bring your grill up to the proper temperature before starting the cooking process. Think of pasta; you wouldn't want to drop the pasta into the water before it's boiling, right?

Before igniting your grill, carefully review the manufacturer recommendations on the types of fuel needed. Gas grills are easy, as there's not much to preheating other than turning on the gas, igniting the sparker, and allowing the temperature gauge to reach proper temperature, which varies depending on what you're grilling.

Wood burning, charcoal, and other solid fuel–burning grills can be a bit trickier, as there are additional factors to consider, such as ambient temperature, moisture, the quality of the grill's metal shell, and often, the lack of a built-in thermometer.

For most charcoal grills, select a bag of regular, self-lighting, Kingsford briquettes. This avoids the use of lighter fluid. Stack a pile of briquettes, about 4 or 5 inches high, that covers about half the grill area. Light the charcoal with a flame, and allow the fire to burn out, uncovered, until you are left with embers or the briquettes ashed over. At this point, cover the grill with the lid for 10 minutes, then your grill will be preheated and ready for use.

Whichever grill you are using, make sure you are always operating the grill in a well-ventilated area (always outdoors, never indoors) and away from anything that has the potential to catch fire from a rogue spark.

Preheating the Electric Smoker

Even though manufacturers may say you don't need to preheat your electric smoker, it's best to have the unit preheated and operational before you're ready to smoke. This process also helps maintain a consistent temperature environment.

Before preheating the smoker being used throughout this book, which is the Smokin Tex Pro-Series Stainless Steel Electric Smoker (page 23), make sure the smoker is stable on a solid foundation. Also choose a dry, sheltered, and well-ventilated location. Do not expose the smoker to any rain or snow.

Prior to plugging the smoker into an outlet, remove the smoking tray and fill three-quarters with dry wood chips. The kind of wood chips depend on what you're smoking (page 17). Don't worry if some of the wood chips fall through the perforation; it won't disrupt anything. Return the tray to the smoker, making sure it is securely in place. (Note: the door will not close if the tray is not properly locked in place.)

Plug the smoker into an outlet, and set the knob on the top of the unit to the desired temperature, depending on what you're smoking. The smoker will be properly preheated when you see a steady stream of white smoke being expelled from the ventilation hole on top of the unit.

MARINATING

Like brining, marinating is a method of soaking food to intensify the flavor while increasing moisture in the food being marinated. Meat, vegetables, seafood, and poultry can all benefit from absorbing marinade. Just make sure to plan ahead so the food has time to marinate. A general rule of thumb is the longer the food marinates, the more flavorful it will become. While beef, pork, and poultry will benefit from marinating 4 to 6 hours and even overnight, some foods like fish and seafood should only marinate for 1 or 2 hours. Any longer and the acid (or citrus) in the marinade will "cook" the fish. Although most marinades are made with a combination of oil, acid (such as citrus, vinegar, or wine), and seasonings, it's worth noting that not all marinades are "wet." Some marinades, often referred to as rubs, can be pastes and dry spice mixtures, which also add flavor to the food.

PAN-FRYING

Pan-frying is similar to sautéing, with a few exceptions. When pan-frying, more fat is used to cook the food and you often cook at lower temperatures. You also won't move the food as much as you would when sautéing. Similar to braising, charring, and roasting, the purpose of pan-frying is to establish a nice, charred crust on the exterior of the food being pan-fried. The partially cooked food is then finished in the oven so the inside can finish cooking.

ROASTING

Roasting, like baking, often occurs in the oven and relies on hot dry air to draw out the natural flavors while cooking the food, such as meat, poultry, and vegetables. Roasting also helps caramelize and char the food, which makes for a crispy outside and moist inside while providing more complex flavors and aromas. Typically when roasting, the food is left uncovered to allow the dry heat to cook the food instead of steam. Roasting is also performed at temperatures ranging from 200°F to 500°F; the food is cooked slowly for a longer period for more tender and juicer results. When roasting at home, be sure to preheat your oven thoroughly at least 30 minutes prior to cooking. You can also use the broiler setting just prior to finishing to boost the overall caramelization of the cooking process.

SAUTÉING

Sautéing is another form of dry-heat cooking that uses a very hot pan and a small amount of fat, such as oil or butter, to cook the food quickly. Like roasting, sautéing also helps brown and caramelize the food, adding more flavor and aroma to the dish. One important rule when sautéing is never to crowd the pan. Too much food in the pan will result in a lower temperature, causing the food to steam rather than cook. When in doubt, use a large sauté pan and sauté in batches, as less is definitely more when it comes to sautéing. Another rule of importance is to keep the food moving. *Sauté* is French and means "to jump," and the more the food moves, the more evenly it will cook.

SEARING

Searing, often performed in a pan with some fat to prevent sticking, is a cooking technique in which high heat produces a charred exterior crust on the food being seared, similar to sautéing. Searing can be performed through baking, braising, grilling, roasting, and sautéing. The primary purpose of searing is to seal in the juices and flavor of the food by forming an attractive outer crust so the juices cannot escape. It is also important to sear all sides of the food. For fresh seafood such as ahi tuna, you may want the inside to be medium rare, so searing only the outside is the trick here. For meats, roasts, and chops, once the exterior has been seared, the meat should be transferred to the oven so the inside, which will still be raw, can finish cooking to your desired temperature.

SMOKING

Smoking is one of the quintessential elements in real barbecue, along with an indirect "low and slow" cooking temperature. Creating and maintaining a consistent temperature is imperative. Also, bringing the smoker up to cooking temperature for at least 30 minutes before adding the food helps ensure you can maintain a consistent temperature environment (page 23). Smoke is also used in other forms of cooking, such as grilling with high heat. The rich smokiness you want to smell and taste should always come from the smoldering wood being used and not the fat or oil drippings or the coals themselves. Wood burning smoke yields superior taste, flavor, and is healthier than any smoke derived from burning fat. When it comes to smoking, patience is the key here, whether cold smoking or hot smoking. For the purpose of this book and the recipes herein, we will be working with hot smoking, which means the smoking process will fully cook the food, as opposed to cold smoking, in which the food is first smoked then cooked and cured before eating.

ALDER

HICKORY

APPLE

OAK

MESQUITE

SMOKING WOODS

You can choose from many varieties of wood when it comes to smoking. What's important, however, is being familiar with the wood spectrum—from mild to strong—and understanding how each wood will affect the food you're smoking. Hardwoods are the wood (or wood chips) you will want to use, as the soft, resinous woods contain too much sap, which produces a heavy smoke not suitable for smoking. Such woods to avoid are cypress, elm, eucalyptus, pine, redwood, fir, spruce, and sycamore. Eastern cedar (not to be confused with untreated Western red cedar, which pairs well with seafood) should also not be used. Also, do not use plywood, construction scraps, or any wood that has been chemically treated. Smoking woods and chips should also be soaked in water, wine, or juice for at least 30 minutes before being placed in the smoker or grill. This helps slow down the burning of the wood while offering additional moisture and flavor. Typically, a few medium-sized pieces of wood or a handful or two of wood chips should be enough to achieve adequate smoke for what you will be smoking in this book.

From a general standpoint, fruit woods like apple, peach, cherry, and pear make excellent smoking woods. They are mild and subtle, offering hints of sweet fruit flavor while providing a delicate smoke to foods like fish and poultry, as well as to pork. Apple is often used when smoking ham while cherry is popular with all meats including beef. Alder is also delicate and sweet and falls at the low end of the smoking spectrum. This wood works particularly well when smoking salmon.

In the middle of the spectrum are woods such as hickory, maple, and oak. Pecan is also in this range and works well when smoking poultry. These middle-spectrum woods offer a medium smoke and pair nicely with pork yet are strong enough to stand up to many cuts of beef. Hickory, which is a little stronger than oak, offers a sweet yet strong bacon-like flavor and is often used when smoking ribs. For small game birds, maple is a pleasant option.

At the other end of the spectrum are the strong woods, like mesquite, olive, and walnut. These woods exude strong earthy flavors and pair well with most red and dark meats. Mesquite, like other woods at the end of the spectrum, should be used in moderation, as it can overpower the food if used excessively. Mesquite is also one of the hottest burning woods. For a lighter version of mesquite, try olive wood, which has a similar flavor to mesquite but is not so heavy on the senses. Walnut, meanwhile, often has a strong and bitter flavor, so mixing it with other woods or wood chips does help to create a milder flavor.

ESSENTIAL EQUIPMENT & TOOLS

Similar to the cooking methods overview in the previous pages, it is equally important to familiarize yourself with some essential equipment and tools to make your life in the kitchen much more pleasurable and efficient while preparing Chef Bugge's fabulous recipes.

BLENDER

The kitchen (or stand up) blender is a must-have when blending dressings, sauces, soups, and more

that should be lump-free. Make sure to invest in a durable, high-performance machine with variable speeds for better productivity and results. Dishwasher-safe parts is also a nice feature to have. Vita-mix and KitchenAid are two reputable brands.

COCKTAIL SHAKER

When looking for a shaker, it is important to get one that feels good to you. A three-piece cobbler shaker that is well built yet still lightweight is recommended. The built-in strainer also means one fewer tool to grab when finishing the cocktail. The Viski cocktail shaker is a solid choice.

FOOD PROCESSOR

Another must-have in the kitchen, the food processor is designed for power, efficiency, and user satisfaction. Look for a professional-grade model that fits easily on the countertop, with a large feed chute and a wide array of user-friendly blades and accessories to choose from. Cuisinart and KitchenAid continue to be reliable among consumers.

GRILL

An outdoor grill is essential when it comes to charring and smoking, and investing in a quality unit will be money well spent. For outdoor gas grills, the Weber seems to remain the best grill on the market with superior performance and its ability to maintain a constant temperature, even during cold or windy conditions. However, most Webers aren't travel-friendly, so investing in an additional portable grill is a good idea, especially if you like to tailgate

or embark on that weekend camping excursion now and again. Gas grills are also an excellent go-to for everyday use, but there are times when certain ingredients call for the charcoal grill. For example, slow cooking certain meats like brisket, tri-tip, or ribs definitely turn out better over charcoal than gas. Weber's inexpensive and always reliable Original Kettle charcoal grill is a must-have alongside the gas grill. For those who like to "set it and forget it" and let the grill work its magic, there are lines of wood-pellet grills on the market that are simple and safe to use. Traeger Grills is one popular and trusted brand that uses wood pellets made with 100 percent pure natural hardwoods for that authentic smoky flavor. There's also the ceramic beast of both a charcoal grill and smoker known as the Big Green Egg, which first appeared in the 1970s. They are excellent at achieving both high temperatures and holding low temperature for smoking. The Big Green Egg can be expensive and is often marketed to those who plan to do *a lot* of cooking. The bottom line here is that there are a lot of grills on the market, so take your time, do your research, and select the grill or grills that best suit your culinary lifestyle.

HIGH-TEMP SPATULA

When introducing a kitchen spatula to hot pans, you sure don't want to be using a rubber spatula that melts or a metal spatula that scratches the pan. The high-temperature spatula is the solution; it includes a silicone blade that's heat resistant to 500° F. Make sure to keep one of these in your kitchen drawer.

ICE CREAM MAKER

Unlike years ago, making ice cream at home is much easier than you might think, thanks to the easy-to-use ice cream makers on the market today. Some ice cream makers even offer settings that let you choose between ice cream, gelato, or sorbet. Invest in a machine that can make at least a couple quarts per batch while having simple controls and various control speeds. Cuisinart has an affordable line of high-quality ice cream makers that are easy for the home cook to operate.

IMMERSION BLENDER

Also known as hand or stick blenders, this piece of equipment is ideal for the kitchen and a very convenient alternative to dragging out that big, lumbering mixer just to whip up a little aioli for a sandwich or marinade for a piece of grilled chicken. Many immersion blenders perform the basic tasks of whipping, blending, and emulsifying, yet are small enough to keep in a kitchen drawer. Make sure to look for one that is stainless steel and offers a couple different speeds. Cuisinart, Hamilton Beach, and KitchenAid are several top-performing immersion blenders on the market.

MEASURING CUPS

Measuring cups are essential in the kitchen to eliminate the guesswork when preparing a recipe. Make sure to invest in a durable set that doesn't feel flimsy and won't bend. Cups with silicone handles are nice to prevent slipping. Longer handles and measurements on the sides are also features that are well appreciated.

MEASURING SPOONS

Many people don't know this, but truth be told: almost all measuring spoons are off by just a little. The US Department of Commerce's National Institute of Standards and Technology (NIST) publishes guidelines for how much tea- and tablespoons should hold. However, not all manufacturers are spot on. Whether round or rectangular measuring spoons (rectangular are great for getting into small spice jars), research online for those brands that have been tested using NIST standards, and try to stay away from those gimmicky sets with unconventional shapes like hearts, color-coded sets, or those labeled a "pinch," "dash," or "smidgen."

MIXING BOWLS

Many at-home cooks probably have a hodge-podge of bowls, collected from those holiday gifts over

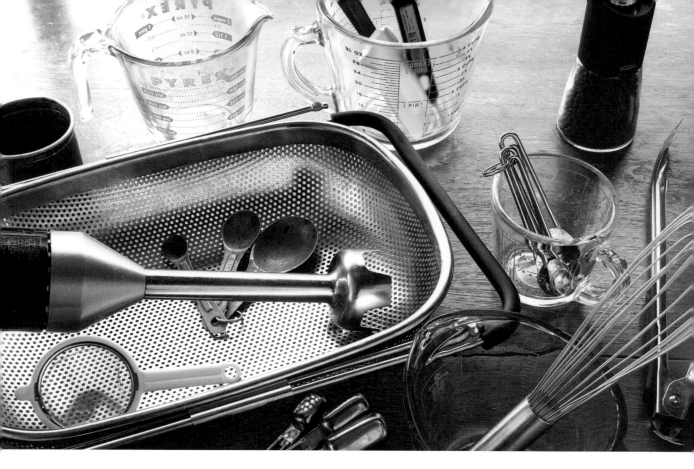

the years, or your great-grandmother's bowls that have finally been passed down to you. Of course, they all work, but for those starting fresh, invest in a classic well-made set made of stainless-steel bowls that are both dishwasher and freezer safe. Wide bowls with slip resistant bottoms and non-toxic plastic lids are added features available today to consider when selecting the perfect bowls for your kitchen.

SAUCE PAN

Well-made models of the sauce pan should reflect superior design, construction, and performance. Look for sauce pans that are made from stainless

steel and are dishwasher safe. Another option are those made with an aluminum core, which heats quickly and allows for even cooking. All-Clad and Cuisinart are two top brands when it comes to high-quality sauce pans.

SAUTÉ PAN

The sauté pan is a wide, flat-bottomed pan with relatively high sides. This pan is not good for searing, but ideal for cooking down greens, shallow frying, and braising. Like all pans, a good sauté pan should heat evenly and feel comfortable and balanced in the hand. Also lean toward the larger-sized pans as opposed to smaller pans.

SMOKER

Like outdoor grills, there are many smokers on the market, including log and wood burning, charcoal, water, pellet, and the good-ol'-fashioned homemade smokers. Rather than dissecting each smoker, the smoker we're going to concentrate on is the smoker used throughout this cookbook and at the restaurant: the Smokin Tex Pro-Series Stainless Steel Electric Smoker. This professional smoker slow cooks without any hassle. You simply plug it in, add the wood and food, shut the door, and set the temperature. It's that easy. Your food will be slow cooked with exact temperature control and without having to constantly tend to the smoker.

SMOKING GUN

This efficient appliance allows you to infuse smoke to a wide variety of foods with ease and without adding any heat. You simply load the gun with wood chips, light, and then direct the smoke tube into whatever container or vessel you're using to add smoke to the desired food. Just a few minutes of smoke and your food will take on that classic smokehouse flavor.

SPICE GRINDER

From flax seeds to coffee beans, having a quality grinder on hand to pulverize ingredients makes life in the kitchen much easier. Look for an electrical grinder (not manual) that is powerful, yet quiet, with steel blades that can handle coffee, nuts, and a variety of spices. Lean toward the larger grinders as opposed to the smaller units.

STOCK POT

The stock pot will perform many tasks in the kitchen, so invest wisely. Look for high-quality construction in either brushed stainless steel or aluminum. Wide bottoms are good, as are cool, secure handles. These pots should heat quickly and evenly while retaining heat whether you're searing, boiling, or canning. All-Clad and Cuisinart make top-of-the-line stock

pots that can go from freezer to stovetop to oven. Be aware, however, that not all stock pots work with induction burners. If you have an induction burner, make sure your stock pot is suitable.

STRAINER/CHINOIS

There are all sorts of strainers on the market, from pasta strainers to soup strainers. Keep a few stainless-steel varieties in your kitchen cupboards. Soup strainers, for example, are excellent to have on hand for basic soup straining. Those with larger openings are also good for homemade jams, compotes, salsas, and sauces, as they work well for mashing fruits and vegetables while removing the skins and seeds. For smoother and even finishes like preparing pea soups, broths, and bouillon, use the chinois-style models.

WHISK

When it comes to whisks, don't buy the first one you see. The whisk you want should offer flex and movement, as many poor-quality whisks are too stiff. The whisk should be sturdy enough to scrape the bottom of the bowl, yet gentle enough to whip up a light salad dressing. Try to avoid those whisks that are heavy, as you don't want your arm getting tired after a minute or two of whisking. Invest in a well-constructed balloon whisk that is comfortable and light in the hand, made of stainless steel, and is dishwasher safe.

RUBS & SEASONINGS

ASIAN SPICE RUB | 27

BARBECUE DRY RUB | 29

BLACKENING SPICE | 30

GRILLED FISH RUB | 32

HARISSA | 33

LATIN RUB | 34

JERK SPICE | 36

PROVENCAL SPICE RUB (HERBS DE PROVENCE) | 37

ASIAN SPICE RUB

MAKES ½ CUP

1 TABLESPOON GROUND STAR
ANISE

½ TEASPOON GROUND FENNEL
SEED

½ TEASPOON FRESH GROUND
BLACK PEPPER

¼ TEASPOON GROUND CLOVES

1 TABLESPOON GROUND
CINNAMON

1 TABLESPOON BROWN SUGAR

1 TABLESPOON KOSHER SALT

2 TABLESPOONS CAYENNE
PEPPER

In a small bowl, combine the star anise, fennel seed, black pepper, cloves, cinnamon, brown sugar, salt, and cayenne pepper. Mix well and store in an airtight container until ready to use. The rub will stay fresh and flavorful for up to 30 days.

BARBECUE DRY RUB

I'm convinced that if we ever have another civil war, it will be triggered by who has the better barbecue. I'm not from the South, yet this debate still manages to find a way into my life, and the argument as to who has the "best" is one, I imagine, that will never stop. We all benefit from this healthy competition of barbecue superiority. We are fortunate to have varieties that cater to our every taste. Starting with a high-quality rub is one of the more important steps in the cooking process as it's the foundation of the flavor profile, and like anything else, a well-built foundation is the key to a successful endeavor. Whenever I make barbecue, someone always asks how much rub I use. The answer is easy: as much as will stick to the meat!

½ CUP BROWN SUGAR

1 TABLESPOON GROUND CUMIN

1 TABLESPOON GROUND BLACK
   PEPPER

1 TEASPOON GROUND
   CORIANDER

1 TABLESPOON KOSHER SALT

2 TABLESPOONS CHILE POWDER

1 TABLESPOON ONION POWDER

1 TABLESPOON GARLIC POWDER

1 TEASPOON CHIPOTLE POWDER

In a small bowl, combine the brown sugar, cumin, black pepper, coriander, salt, chile powder, onion powder, garlic powder, and chipotle powder. Mix well and store in an airtight container until ready to use. The rub will stay fresh and flavorful for up to 30 days.

BLACKENING SPICE

MAKES 1/2 CUP

Before I was able to expand my culinary horizon, the notion of intentionally burning food seemed foreign to me. I attended a French culinary school, where it was religiously taught that if it's burnt, throw it out. I was young and impressionable and thought French style was the only way of making it in the world. Oh, to be young and naïve again. French cooking is, no doubt, the benchmark for what the mass consumer expects haute cuisine to be. The decadence, the sophistication, the elegance, and the romance behind Parisian food is infatuating. But it is not the only way to cook. Take blackening, for example. This is a creole technique from the South, which does have very deep French roots in which the true form of blackening comes from using traditional blackening spices in a very high-heat cast-iron pan. The results are equally divine.

---

1 TABLESPOON SMOKED
   PAPRIKA
1 TEASPOON CAYENNE PEPPER
1 TEASPOON DRY OREGANO
1 TABLESPOON GARLIC POWDER
1 TABLESPOON ONION POWDER
1 TABLESPOON DRY GROUND
   THYME
1 TABLESPOON FRESH GROUND
   BLACK PEPPER
1 TABLESPOON KOSHER SALT

In a small bowl, combine the smoked paprika, cayenne pepper, dry oregano, garlic powder, onion powder, thyme, black pepper, and salt. Mix well and store in an airtight container until ready to use. The rub will stay fresh and flavorful for up to 30 days.

GRILLED FISH RUB

MAKES 1/4 CUP

Adding rubs to seafood, especially fish, can be tricky. Fish have a delicate flavor so adding too many elements will quickly overpower that fresh fish taste. Now, if you are looking to mask the taste of that bargain tilapia you got on sale, by all means, go all-out. But if you are looking to highlight the subtleties of, say, market-fresh halibut, then proceed with caution and use the rub as a complementary component rather than an overwhelming rub.

1 TABLESPOON SMOKED
    PAPRIKA
1 TABLESPOON ALEPPO POWDER
1 TEASPOON GROUND CUMIN
1 TEASPOON GROUND
    CORIANDER
½ TEASPOON GARLIC POWDER
1 TEASPOON KOSHER SALT
1 TEASPOON FRESH GROUND
    BLACK PEPPER
CANOLA OIL, AS NEEDED

In a small bowl, combine the smoked paprika, Aleppo powder, cumin, coriander, garlic powder, salt, and pepper. Mix well and transfer to an airtight container. The rub will stay fresh and flavorful for up to 30 days.

When ready to use, combine the seasoning mixture with some canola oil to create a slurry paste. Then rub liberally on both sides of the fish before grilling.

HARISSA
MAKES 1/2 CUP

Hailing from North Africa, Harissa is one of those versatile sauces that's handy to keep around "just in case." Originally from Tunisia, thought to be a product of the Columbia Exchange in 1500s, Harissa has carved its way in as a dietary staple. Although the marinade has many variations, the base almost always consists of red peppers, olive oil, garlic, and chilies. One of the many pleasures I get from being a chef is having the resources to explore other culture's cuisines. Even if I don't have the opportunity to travel to a certain region of the world, I can almost always find someone in my vicinity who is proficient in a type of cuisine that I am researching. I worked next to a man some years ago who was born and raised in Tunisia and first introduced me to Harissa. Now, I almost always have a fresh jar of Harissa around to put on my eggs at home, or brunch potatoes at the restaurant, along with countless other uses. Try it. I'll bet you'll like it.

---

8 DRY GUAJILLO OR ANCHO PEPPERS

4 GARLIC CLOVES

1 TEASPOON KOSHER SALT

3 TABLESPOONS EXTRA-VIRGIN OLIVE OIL

1½ TEASPOONS GROUND CORIANDER

1 TEASPOON GROUND CUMIN

ZEST FROM 1 LIME

1 TEASPOON LIME JUICE

Preheat the oven to 400°F.

Place the peppers in the oven for 10 minutes. Remove and transfer the peppers to a hot-water bath for 20 minutes. Remove from the water and take out the seeds and stems.

Place in a food processer or blender, and add the peppers along with the garlic, salt, olive oil, coriander, cumin, lime zest, and lime juice. Blend until the mixture forms a smooth paste. Store in an airtight container in the refrigerator until ready to use. The rub will stay fresh and flavorful for up to 1 week.

LATIN RUB

MAKES 1/2 CUP

Every culture around the world can be defined by a certain combination of flavors. Whether it's *ras el hanout* from north Africa, *five spice* from China, or *herbs de provence* from southern France, when certain flavors are paired together, it makes the region of origin more easily identifiable. Many diners have this ability without even knowing it. For example, when cumin, coriander, fenugreek, turmeric, and peppers are combined, many of us will immediately think, "Indian food!" Just so happens the combination of flavors I described is more commonly called curry. While many cultures, mainly around the southeast Asia region, have their own versions of curry, it is more commonly associated with Indian cuisine. Latin spices, like many other demographics around the world, are very regional, meaning they vary greatly from one country to another. The climate in northern Mexico is vastly different from southern Mexico, so it would make sense that each region has different products available to them. However, the entire Latin region can agree on a few flavors. Chiles, like pasilla, cascabel, ancho, chile de arbol, and chipotle are peppers widely found in Latin cuisine. These peppers, often paired with flavors like oregano, cumin, coriander, and cilantro, create a combination that many people would associate with Latin cuisine.

¼ CUP GROUND CUMIN

2 TABLESPOONS GROUND
    CORIANDER

1 TABLESPOON GROUND CHILE
    POWDER

1 TEASPOON CAYENNE POWDER

1 TABLESPOON KOSHER SALT

1 TEASPOON GROUND BLACK
    PEPPER

ZEST FROM 1 LIME

In a small bowl, combine the cumin, coriander, chile powder, cayenne powder, salt, black pepper, and lime zest. Mix well and store in an airtight container until ready to use. The rub will stay fresh and flavorful for up to 1 week.

JERK SPICE

MAKES 1/2 CUP

The term *jerk* comes from the word *jerking,* which is in reference to poking holes in the meat so the flavor of the rub can be easily absorbed. For those fortunate enough to have traveled to the island country of Jamaica, this national dish is prepared with such respect that one is almost envious of the preparation. The traditional fire pits once used for creating true jerk-style proteins have evolved into halved oil drums, but the flavors have remained true. If you are preparing this at home, any gas or wood-burning grill will work great.

---

1 TABLESPOON CAYENNE POWDER

1 TABLESPOON GARLIC POWDER

1 TABLESPOON ONION POWDER

2 TEASPOONS DRY THYME LEAVES

1 TABLESPOON GRANULATED SUGAR

1½ TEASPOONS SMOKED PAPRIKA

1 TEASPOON ALLSPICE

1 TEASPOON FRESH GROUND BLACK PEPPER

1 TABLESPOON KOSHER SALT

¼ TEASPOON CINNAMON

½ TEASPOON FRESH GROUND NUTMEG

In a small bowl, combine the cayenne powder, garlic powder, onion powder, dry thyme leaves, sugar, smoked paprika, allspice, black pepper, salt, cinnamon, and ground nutmeg. Mix well and transfer to an airtight container. The rub will stay fresh and flavorful for up to 30 days.

PROVENCAL SPICE RUB (HERBS DE PROVENCE)

MAKES 1¼ CUPS

"You can't make flavor in a pot." I worked for a chef who taught this mantra like religion. What he meant was, it is unrealistic to add a bunch of seasoning to a finished pot of food and expect it to live up to its full potential. You must develop flavor from the moment you decide to make the dish. In professional kitchens, this means every step must be carried out. Properly salting water when cooking pasta is a great example. If you don't properly season the water, your result will never be as good as it can be. Unlike its name suggests, *Herbs de Provence* is not a certain herb mix used only in a certain region but rather a commonly used mix of herbs in Provence in the southeast region of France. Herbs de Provence typically contains a base of savory, marjoram, rosemary, thyme, and oregano. This is one of the few premixed herbs I always stock in my home pantry. The combination of savory herbs also works well as a rub when grilling meats.

¼ CUP FRESH SAGE, MINCED

2 TABLESPOONS CILANTRO
   STEMS, MINCED

⅓ CUP GARLIC, MINCED

ZEST FROM 2 LIMES

¼ CUP KOSHER SALT

¼ CUP FRESH GROUND BLACK
   PEPPER

In a small bowl, combine the sage, cilantro, garlic, lime zest, salt, and pepper. Mix well and store in the refrigerator until ready to use. The rub will stay fresh and flavorful for up to 1 week.

DRESSINGS, MARINADES & SAUCES

BLACKENED TOMATO SALSA | 39

BLOOD ORANGE GASTRIQUE | 42

BULGOGI MARINADE | 43

BURNT ASH AIOLI | 44

CARNE ASADA MARINADE (WITH FLANK STEAK) | 46

CHARRED ONION SOUBISE | 48

CLASSIC STEAK MARINADE | 49

GRILLED PINEAPPLE SALSA | 50

GRILLED SHRIMP MARINADE | 51

MOLE NEGRO | 52

SMOKED AVOCADO EMULSION | 54

SMOKED RADISH GREEN AIOLI | 56

BLACKENED TOMATO SALSA
MAKES 2 CUPS

I consider myself truly blessed to have been raised by my parents. My mother would wake up early every morning to prepare my sister and me breakfast, and I don't mean pour us cereal or put some frozen waffles in the toaster. She would actually prepare breakfast. That meant we would wake up to the fragrant aromas of grilled tomatoes, garlic, and jalapeños on the *plancha* (griddle) as mom prepped her homemade salsa. The scents of fresh masa for tortillas and reheated beans from the night before also permeated the kitchen. By the time we made our way to the table, there was a spread of Blackened Tomato Salsa, fresh cheese, eggs, tortillas, and beans. I will admit this may not sound appealing to every child, but to me, it was heaven. Smell is the sense most attached to memory, so to this day, whenever I smell Latin aromatics charring, I'm instantly taken back to childhood. Without question, salsa in my culture is a staple. Let me rephrase that, salsa in my culture is *the* staple. Never will you partake in a Mexican meal where there is not a form of this spiced condiment present at the table. After all, salsa is great on virtually everything.

---

2 POUNDS FRESH RED TOMATOES

6 CLOVES PEELED GARLIC

½ LARGE YELLOW ONION, OUTER SKIN REMOVED AND CUT INTO QUARTERS

1 TABLESPOON DRY CORIANDER

1 TEASPOON CUMIN

1 TEASPOON BLACK PEPPERCORNS

2 TABLESPOONS OLIVE OIL

ZEST AND JUICE FROM 1 LIME

1 TABLESPOON SALT

Preheat the oven to 450°F.

On a sheet pan, lay out the tomatoes, garlic, onion, coriander, cumin, and peppercorns. Roast in the oven until the tomatoes have developed a charred skin, about 15 minutes, depending on whether you have a conventional or convection oven. This can also be done in a sauté pan by heating a dry sauté pan over medium-high heat, adding the tomatoes, and toasting until very dark. Then remove and, using the same pan, add the garlic, onions, coriander, cumin, and peppercorns over medium heat until they become very aromatic. Once the tomatoes are charred and everything else is toasted, add the ingredients to a blender, along with the olive oil, lime zest and juice, and salt. Pulse on high until well blended. Store in a sealed container in the refrigerator until ready to use. The salsa will stay fresh and flavorful for up to 1 week.

Blackened Tomato Salsa

BLOOD ORANGE GASTRIQUE
MAKES 1 1/2 CUPS

Almost every culture has their own version of a gastrique, which is simply a sweet-and-sour sauce with a syrup-like consistency. Gastriques are one of those sauces in a chef's arsenal just like vinaigrettes. This amazingly simple sauce can turn a pedestrian dish into something served at a five-star restaurant. Burnt sugar combined with an acid (in most cases vinegar) creates depths of flavor that hits multiple parts of the palate. This recipe is a Blood Orange Gastrique, which pairs astonishingly well with fresh shellfish, such as scallops. Once you have mastered this version, I strongly urge you to experiment with other gastriques using different combinations of sweet and sour ingredients.

---

1 CUP WHITE SUGAR

½ CUP WATER

½ CUP SHERRY VINEGAR

½ CUP BLOOD ORANGE JUICE

In a heavy-bottomed sauce pot over medium heat, add the sugar and water to dissolve the sugar. At first, the edges of the pot that are the hottest will start to turn brown from being burned. Very carefully, and I do mean carefully, stir the sugar so that it burns equally. Once the sugar is the color of a brown paper bag, add both the vinegar and orange juice. Immediately, the caramelized sugar will harden—don't panic! You have just introduced cold ingredients to the scalding liquid sugar, returning it to its original solid state. Continue to stir, allowing the mixture to return to a liquid so it becomes one homogenous mix. Once the entire pot is liquid again, very carefully transfer the mixture into a metal bowl and place in the refrigerator to cool. Once cool, remove and drizzle the gastrique over almost anything. It's basically adult liquid candy. Once you try it, you will understand what I mean. Enjoy!

BULGOGI MARINADE
MAKES ¾ CUP

Bulgogi is one of my favorite marinades to keep on hand, and one I make sure to remember off the top of my head. It's also very versatile. While usually reserved for beef or pork, I've found Bulgogi tastes great on a variety of proteins. For this recipe, I prefer to use flank steak or skirt steak, but feel free to use on anything you have available.

¼ CUP HIGH-QUALITY SESAME OIL

2 TABLESPOONS MINCED GARLIC

2 TABLESPOONS MINCED SHALLOT

1 TEASPOON GROUND BLACK PEPPER

⅓ CUP SOY SAUCE

1 TABLESPOON SUGAR

¼ CUP CHOPPED SCALLIONS

2 TABLESPOONS SESAME SEEDS

2 TABLESPOONS MIRIN

In a bowl, combine the sesame oil, garlic, shallot, pepper, soy sauce, sugar, scallions, sesame seeds, and mirin. Mix well.

Massage the marinade into your desired protein. Allow the protein to sit in the marinade in the refrigerator for at least 2 hours, up to 24 hours. Grill the protein at a high temperature for a short period of time. Caramelization of the sugars is the desired result here. If the pan or grill you use is too low in temperature, your result will look like that of boiled meat and the flavor profile will not turn out as well.

BURNT ASH AIOLI

MAKES 2 ¼ CUPS

The restaurant world is conquered and lost on how you manage your margins. The margins are so minimal that we are continually finding ways to improve our bottom line. Having the ability to think outside the box, both as a professional chef and home cook, will greatly impress your guests, whether it be family, friends, or paying patrons. One such example is this unique aioli made from burning greens. It is an example of complete utilization while offering a new dish to enhance the dining experience.

½-POUND GREENS THAT WOULD
    OTHERWISE BE DISCARDED
    (SCALLION TOPS SEEM TO
    WORK THE BEST)
ZEST FROM 1 LIME
1 TEASPOON SALT
2 CUPS NEUTRAL OIL (CANOLA)
3 LARGE EGG YOLKS
1 TEASPOON LEMON JUICE

Preheat the oven to 425°F.

Using a sheet pan, dry-roast the greens until they are completely dehydrated and black (about 20 minutes). Don't be afraid to burn them—this is what you want. Remove from oven and let cool.

In a blender, add the burnt greens along with the lime zest and salt. Purée while slowly adding the oil until well emulsified. Set aside.

In a food processor or another blender, emulsify the egg yolks and lemon juice for 1 minute. Then slowly add to the burnt greens mixture until the consistency is that of a creamy aioli.

Note: If you find the aioli too thick, simply add a few dashes of water to thin out the mixture.

CARNE ASADA MARINADE
(WITH FLANK STEAK)
MAKES 3 CUPS

Growing up in a Mexican household, Latin flavors were dominant in our nightly cuisine. One of my favorite dishes was Carne Asada. The bold flavors from the chilies paired with the subtleties from the floral components charred on the backyard barbecue was such a palate pleaser that I was able to appreciate the meal even at a young age. The simplicity from the marinade makes this user-friendly to anyone yet easily produces a restaurant-quality result. The key to success here is the word *marinade*. Commit to letting the meat sit in the marinade at least overnight for optimal results. I promise it's worth the wait.

---

1 TABLESPOON GROUND CUMIN

1 TABLESPOON SMOKED PAPRIKA

1 TABLESPOON GROUND BLACK PEPPER

6 GARLIC CLOVES, PEELED AND MINCED

1 CUP ORANGE JUICE

¾ CUP LIME JUICE

¼ CUP SOY SAUCE

¼ CUP CHOPPED CILANTRO

¾ CUP CANOLA OIL

8 OUNCES DARK MEXICAN BEER (MODELO NEGRO)

5 POUNDS FLANK STEAK (OR SKIRT STEAK)

TORTILLAS

GUACAMOLE

In a small bowl, add the cumin, smoked paprika, black pepper, and minced garlic. Mix well to combine. In another (larger) bowl, add the orange juice, lime juice, soy sauce, cilantro, oil, and beer. Mix well to combine.

Massage the "dry" ingredients from the small bowl onto both sides of the flank or skirt steak, and transfer to a deep-sided dish, such as a glass baking dish. Next, pour the "wet" ingredients from the larger bowl over the top of the meat. Toss the meat a couple times to evenly coat. Cover firmly with plastic wrap and let marinate in the refrigerate, preferably overnight, but a minimum of 6 hours.

Grill the marinated flank steak, about 6 minutes on each side for medium rare. Remove from heat and serve warm with fresh tortillas and guacamole.

CHARRED ONION SOUBISE

MAKES 2 CUPS

Onions are one those simple foods seldom thought to be the main component of a dish. Most often they are an afterthought, added to a pan or sauce to accompany the star of the show. What I enjoy about Charred Onion Soubise is that the recipe is very easy to make while transforming a pedestrian item like a yellow onion into a classical French sauce to impress family and friends.

---

1 POUND YELLOW ONIONS

3 TABLESPOONS UNSALTED
    BUTTER

¼ CUP ALL-PURPOSE FLOUR

1 CUP WHOLE MILK

½ CUP FRESHLY GRATED
    PARMESAN CHEESE

½ TEASPOON FRESHLY GRATED
    NUTMEG

Preheat an outdoor grill (page 10).

Peel the onions and cut into ½-inch-thick discs. Places the onions on the grill and allow to char on one side. Carefully turn over and char the other side. Remove from the grill and place the onions in a bowl. Cover with aluminum foil and set in a warm place to allow to steam for 20 minutes, then dice the onions and set aside. Next, melt the butter in a saucepan over medium heat. Add the flour and stir constantly until the "roux" begins to smell nutty. Add the milk and onions and bring to a boil, then reduce to a simmer on low heat. Simmer for about 12 minutes, stirring every couple of minutes so the mixture doesn't stick to the pan. To finish, fold in the Parmesan cheese and nutmeg. Season to taste and reserve until ready to use.

CLASSIC STEAK MARINADE
MAKES 1 1/2 CUPS

Regardless of what cut of beef is in your budget—Ribeye, New York, Filet Mignon, Sirloin—any steak can benefit from adding a little flavor to the meat. This is a simple recipe made mostly with common pantry ingredients. Should you find yourself missing an item or two, don't panic; so long as you have salt, the marinade will still turn out.

⅓ CUP EXTRA-VIRGIN OLIVE OIL

¼ CUP RED WINE VINEGAR

2 TABLESPOONS
   WORCESTERSHIRE SAUCE

1 LARGE MINCED SHALLOT

1 TABLESPOON MINCED THYME

1 TEASPOON MINCED ROSEMARY

1 TEASPOON DRY MUSTARD

1 TABLESPOON KOSHER SALT

1 TABLESPOON FRESH GROUND
   BLACK PEPPER

In a bowl, combine the olive oil, vinegar, Worcestershire, shallot, thyme, rosemary, dry mustard, salt, and pepper. Mix well. Refrigerate in an airtight container until ready to use. The marinade will stay fresh and flavorful for up to 1 week.

When ready to use, coat your desired cut of steak evenly with the marinade and refrigerate for up to 12 hours. Do not wipe off the marinade before grilling.

GRILLED PINEAPPLE SALSA

MAKES 3 CUPS

Garnishes are culinary accessories that can take a meal from good to great. Or a restaurant from respectable to phenomenal. Garnishes, if you're not familiar, are the side components we add to a dish to complement the star of the meal. They can be as simple as a fresh sprig of mint or as complex as a thousand-day sauce. Either way, garnishes are essential in elevating one's cuisine. Take a taco, for example. Everyone has had one in their life at one point or another. Let's say that taco is filled with fresh shrimp. Eaten alone, just shrimp and a tortilla, the taco would be tasty I'm sure, but why settle for just tasty? Let's add that magical "aha" moment the next time the food touches our palate. This is where garnishes come in. Take that same taco, but this time grill some pineapple, roast some cabbage, char a jalapeño and some onions, toss it together, and there you have it. You have achieved that "aha" moment! You have just transcended the simplicity of pedestrian food that has plagued us for far too long and elevated, in this case, the taco to a new level. Next time you think about preparing a meal, envision the dish in your mind, imagine the flavors in your mouth, and give some thought as to what the meal may need to take it to that next level.

- 1 LARGE RIPE PINEAPPLE
- 1 Fresno chile
- 1 TABLESPOON LIME JUICE
- 1 TEASPOON LIME ZEST
- ¼ MINCED CILANTRO
- 2 TABLESPOONS RICE WINE VINEGAR
- 2 TABLESPOONS AGAVE SYRUP
- 1 TEASPOON KOSHER SALT
- 1 TEASPOON FRESH CRACKED BLACK PEPPER
- ¼ CUP QUESO FRESCO, COTIJA, OR FETA CHEESE (OPTIONAL)

Preheat an outdoor grill (page 10).

Using a sharp knife, carefully cut the top and bottom off the end of the pineapple. Stand the pineapple up and slice off the skin. Next, cut long slices down the middle, about ¼ inch thick. Transfer the slices of pineapple to the grill, and grill for 3 minutes. Turn the slices at a 45-degree angle, and grill for another 3 minutes. Turn the slices over and repeat. Remove the slices from the grill and place in a covered container for 20 minutes to allow the pineapple to steam and break down. Meanwhile, remove the tops and seeds from the chile and mince. In a bowl, combine the minced chile with the lime juice, lime zest, cilantro, vinegar, agave syrup, salt, and pepper. Mix well. Once cool, cut the pineapple into ¼-inch-squares. Add the pineapple and toss with the rest of the ingredients. Reserve or refrigerate until ready to use.

GRILLED SHRIMP MARINADE
MAKES ¾ CUP

The first time I took over a kitchen and was allowed full autonomy over a menu, I made sure to keep my mentor on speed dial at all times. I would work tirelessly to make sure those first few menus were as good as they could be. Whenever I thought a menu was ready, I would send the menu off to my mentor to proofread. One day, my mentor asked me, "How come you never use prawns? You live in Washington state and have the some of the best prawns in the world!" To be honest, I never featured prawns because I was nervous to cook with them, as they can be difficult. Just a tad overcooked, and they become a rubbery vessel. Nevertheless, I soon began to buy prawns in bulk so I could take them home and try different flavors, temperatures, and techniques until I was pleased with a dish that I was proud to serve to family and friends. Here's one of those recipes.

½ CUP EXTRA-VIRGIN OLIVE OIL

2 TABLESPOONS MINCED GARLIC

1 SMALL MINCED SHALLOT

1 TABLESPOON CHAMPAGNE VINEGAR

2 TABLESPOONS CHOPPED TARRAGON

1 TEASPOON KOSHER SALT

In a bowl, combine the olive oil, garlic, shallot, champagne vinegar, tarragon, and salt. Mix well. Toss a liberal amount of the marinade with the desired amount of peeled and deveined prawns. Refrigerate for 2 hours, up to 12 hours.

Using wooden skewers that have been presoaked in water, or metal skewers, impale the prawns to make them into half-moon shapes; this will help with the grilling process. Preheat an outdoor grill (page 10). Place the skewers on the grill perpendicular to the grating, and cook for 1½ to 2 minutes per side. Prawns are cooked when the entirety of the outer flesh has turned pink. Garnish with Grilled Pineapple Salsa (page 50).

MOLE NEGRO

MAKES 5 QUARTS

Washington state, where I live, has a large population of migrant workers. In these communities, you can experience some of the best Latin cuisine outside of their respective countries. Tacos, pupusas, gallo pinto, or menudo—you are sure to find some of the very best here. There is a small eatery in Ballard, just outside of Seattle, called *El Camion,* which is a personal favorite of mine. I'm convinced the mole they use is one of those recipes that has been passed down from generation to generation. Mole is a staple in Oaxacan cuisine. In this approachable version, you can use this mole to make chicken with mole, enchiladas, or chile rellenos.

---

1 POUND DRIED ANCHO CHILIES

½ POUND DRIED CASCABEL CHILIES

2 TABLESPOONS FRESH THYME

2 TABLESPOONS CUMIN

2 TABLESPOONS CORIANDER SEED

5 CLOVES

1 TABLESPOON GROUND CINNAMON

1 POUND SALTED BUTTER

2 CUPS PEELED AND ROUGHLY CHOPPED CARROTS

2 CUPS ROUGHLY CHOPPED WHITE ONIONS

2 CUPS CHOPPED TOMATOES

8 CLOVES PEELED GARLIC

½ CUP SESAME SEEDS

2 CUPS CHOPPED ALMONDS

4 OUNCES MEXICAN CHOCOLATE

4 QUARTS CHICKEN STOCK (OR VEGETABLE OR BEEF)

Preheat the oven to 400°F.

Place the dried chilies on a baking sheet and roast in the oven for 15 minutes, or until the chilies are very aromatic and have an almost burnt-like quality. Remove from the oven and set aside to cool.

Next, add the thyme, cumin, coriander, cloves, and cinnamon to a baking sheet and roast in the oven for 2 or 3 minutes to activate the flavors. Remove from the oven and set aside.

In a large stock pot over medium heat, melt the butter. Once melted, add the carrots, onions, tomatoes, and garlic, and let sweat, stirring occasionally, until the vegetables caramelize. While the vegetables are cooking, de-seed and remove the tops from the roasted chilies. Then add the chilies to the stock pot. Next, add the roasted spices, along with the sesame seeds and almonds. Continue to cook over medium heat, stirring constantly, for about 5 additional minutes. Next, add the chocolate and stock. Bring to a boil and reduce to a simmer for 1 hour. Set aside entire pot and let cool.

Note: If you have an immersion blender, you can purée the entire batch. Otherwise, pour small batches of the cooled mixture into a kitchen blender and purée. Once puréed, strain and keep cool until ready to serve.

SMOKED AVOCADO EMULSION

MAKES ¾ CUP

Avocadoes are very prominent in my life; they make an appearance at almost every meal. Over the last two decades, avocadoes have exploded onto the culinary scene in a large way. Nowadays, if you open a restaurant and you don't have some sort of avocado option or add-on, you've missed the bus. With the interest in healthy eating at an all-time high, the demand for these berries (yes, avocadoes are berries) has led to an inflated price we're not used to. That's because the avocado is one of Mother Nature's finer creations. It's so versatile. Not many fruits or vegetables can be transformed in the ways avocadoes can and still be delicious. Raw, grilled, smoked, or puréed, avocados are always satisfying.

This emulsion using the celebrated avocado is fabulous as a sandwich spread,
a base for guacamole, or a simple garnish on a salad.

---

2 AVOCADOS

½ TEASPOON LIME ZEST

1 TEASPOON LIME JUICE

1 SMALL PEELED SHALLOT

½ TEASPOON SALT

**½ TEASPOON GROUND
CORIANDER**

**1 TEASPOON EXTRA-VIRGIN
OLIVE OIL**

1 TEASPOON KOSHER SALT

Preheat an outdoor smoker (page 12).

Carefully halve and remove the pit from each avocado. Using a spoon, remove pieces of the avocado flesh and place on a smoking tray. Smoke on high for 10 minutes. Remove from smoker and add the avocado pieces to a food processor or blender along with the lime zest, lime juice, shallot, salt, coriander, olive oil, and salt. Pulse on high until the entire mix is emulsified into one homogenous mixture. Strain the mixture to remove any solids and chill until ready to use.

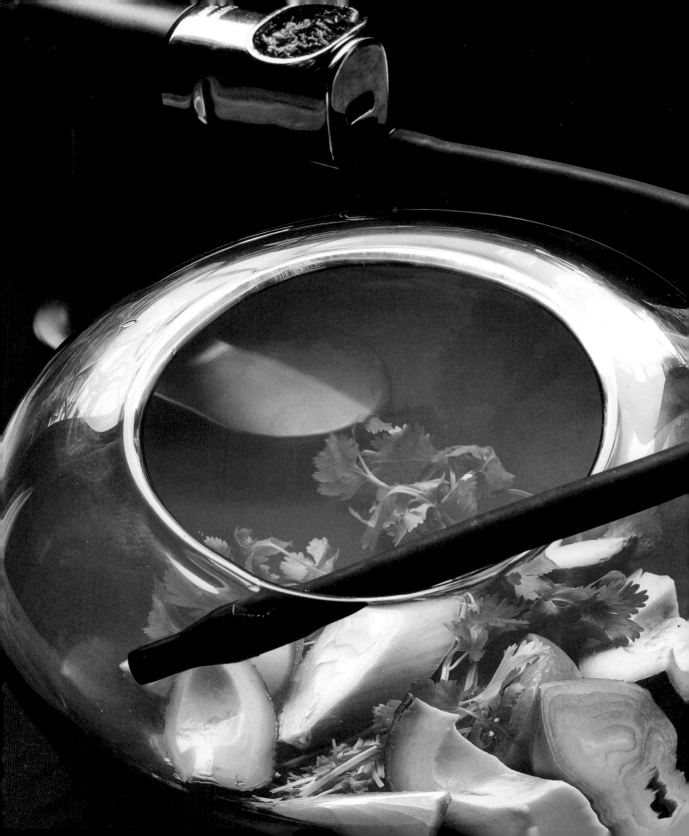

SMOKED RADISH GREEN AIOLI

MAKES 4 CUPS

In a professional kitchen, we are always trying to find new and innovative ways to utilize products that would otherwise get thrown away or be thought of as scrap. Here, we have found a creative way to use the tops of fresh radishes, which most people wouldn't give a second thought to, making them into a creamy, smoky sauce that works as an excellent complementary component to almost any dish.

---

4 BUNCHES RADISH GREENS (CLEANED AND BLANCHED)

ZEST FROM 1 LIME

1 TEASPOON SALT

3 CUPS NEUTRAL OIL (CANOLA)

4 LARGE EGG YOLKS

1 TEASPOON LEMON JUICE

Rinse the radish greens well, blanch them in boiling salted water for 30 seconds, then place them immediately into an ice-water bath to stop the cooking process. Strain.

After blanching the radish greens, you want to preheat the smoker to 200°F, place them on a tray suitable for the smoker, and smoke for 20 minutes.

In a blender, add the radish greens, along with the lime zest and salt. Slowly add the oil and purée until well emulsified. Set aside.

In a food processor or another blender, and the egg yolks and lemon juice and emulsify for 1 minute. Then slowly add to the emulsified radish mixture until the consistency is that of a creamy aioli.

Note: If you find the aioli too thick, simply add a few dashes of water to thin out the mixture.

THE MENU
FIERY COCKTAILS & SPIRITS

CHARRED LIME MARGARITA | 58

FIERY COFFEE | 61

GRILLED PEACH SANGRIA | 62

JET BLACK MANHATTAN | 64

LATIN CONFUSION | 66

SMOKED AGAVE | 66

SMOKED DAIQUIRI | 67

SMOKED OLD FASHIONED | 68

SMOKY SAZERAC | 68

CHARRED LIME MARGARITA
MAKES 1 COCKTAIL [3 OUNCES]

The margarita, the go-to drink for many partygoers and socialites. With hundreds of variations, this cocktail has created a legacy around the world that is sure to last indefinitely. I was in a small town in the Netherlands last year having dinner on a patio that could have very easily been mistaken for someone's backyard, when I noticed the restaurant had five different kinds of margaritas on the menu. With a cocktail as versatile as this, take the opportunity to make the margarita your own. Play with smoking and charring different components of the drink and see what you can come up with. Sometimes I also like to spritz the top of the finished cocktail with a little herbal spirit spray, such as Butterfly Spray from Wild Earth. This can be purchased online and offers essential oils of cypress, orange, and lavender along with a dazzling purple hue. There are really no rules when it comes to margaritas. I've tasted many that were delicious and unique, and some that were unique yet not too savory. Worse comes to worse, you will fall into the latter, but it's better to try and fail than to never have tried at all.

---

2 OUNCES PREMIUM SILVER TEQUILA

½ OUNCE COINTREAU

1 OUNCE CHARRED LIME JUICE (RECIPE ON PAGE 60)

¼ OUNCE AGAVE SYRUP

CHARRED LIME WEDGE, HERBAL SPIRIT SPRAY (GARNISH, OPTIONAL)

In a cocktail shaker filled with ice, add the tequila, Cointreau, Charred Lime Juice, and agave syrup. Shake vigorously and strain into a cocktail glass filled with ice. Garnish with a charred lime wedge and a spritz or two of herbal spirit spray, if desired.

CHARRED LIME JUICE

2 LIMES, HALVED

Preheat a cast-iron pan over medium heat.

Place the limes, flesh side down, on the pan. Allow the limes to caramelize on the one side for 1 to 2 minutes. Remove from pan and allow to cool. Squeeze the juice from the charred limes and strain into a small container.

FIERY COFFEE
MAKES 1 COCKTAIL (9 OUNCES)

The combination of everyday food or drink mixed with fire for the sake of showmanship can undoubtedly be an entertaining notion. Many of us have, at some point, been to a bar and witnessed cocktails being lit on fire, and been wowed by the whole ordeal. A little showmanship can go a long way when it comes to entertaining. Knowing a few parlor tricks is a surefire way to keep your guests engaged. A word of warning, however: Working with fire and flame can be dangerous. Always proceed with caution.

2 OUNCES 151-PROOF RUM

2 OUNCES COFFEE LIQUEUR

3 OUNCES ESPRESSO

RIM: 1 LIME WEDGE AND 1 OR
     2 TEASPOONS SUGAR

WHIPPED CREAM AND
     CINNAMON (GARNISH)

Using a wine glass, glass coffee mug, or Irish coffee mug, wet the rim of the glass with the wedge of lime and dust the rim with sugar. Pour the rum into the glass. Tilt the glass slightly in your hand, and VERY CAREFULLY, set the alcohol on fire using a long lighter or match. Swirl the glass around in your hand for a few seconds to caramelize the rim of the glass. Gently pour in the coffee liqueur, espresso, and stir gently. Garnish with a dollop of whipped cream and sprinkle of cinnamon.

GRILLED PEACH SANGRIA

MAKES 1 QUART

My love affair with sangria began while spending time with my cousins in southern Mexico. During one warm night, we were on our way to see a movie when we came across an Argentinian steakhouse nestled between the movie theater and a shoe store. We decided to try the restaurant before heading into the theater. I remember the waiter recommending the sangria to start, so we indulged. I can still recall the handblown clear glass pitcher with aqua trim like it was yesterday. I also vividly remember the aroma of the Malbec saturated with fresh apples and lime-rimmed glasses. To this day, I remember the taste of that first sip. Had it not been for that night many years ago, there's a possibility I may have never tried sangria because of the misconception that it is not masculine to partake in such beverages as sangria. I couldn't disagree more.

---

4 RIPE PEACHES

1 BOTTLE HIGH-QUALITY WHITE WINE (SAUVIGNON BLANC)

1 WHOLE LEMON, HALVED

1 CUP GRANULATED SUGAR

½ CUP COINTREAU

ORANGE SLICES (GARNISH)

Preheat an outdoor grill (page 10).

Quarter the peaches and place flesh-side down on the grill. Allow the peaches to char on all three sides (two inner flesh and outer skin). Remove from grill and allow to cool. In a stock pot over medium-high heat, add the white wine, two lemon halves, sugar, and Cointreau. Bring to a boil. Immediately reduce to a simmer and allow to continue simmering for 20 minutes. Remove from heat. Cut each quarter of the peach in half and add to the sangria mixture. Transfer to the refrigerator and let sit overnight. When ready to serve, pour over ice and garnish with orange slices.

JET BLACK MANHATTAN
MAKES 1 COCKTAIL (3 OUNCES)

Understanding when, and how, to use activated charcoal in your food and drink can be a valuable resource when entertaining guests. What if you could turn almost any food black with just a dash of powder without ever changing the flavor profile? Sounds like it might be fun, right? It is, so long as you don't go too far. When activated charcoal first hit the market, I tried to get ahead of the curve and went dramatically overboard with my experimentations. The unfortunate benefactor of these experiments was usually my wife, who did not appreciate being served black scrambled eggs with black buttered toast and black cottage cheese served on a black plate. Remember, everything in moderation. The next time you're mixing drinks, and a little charcoal to the cocktail and watch your guest's reaction. It will be worth it.

2 OUNCES PREMIUM RYE
    WHISKEY
1 OUNCE AVERNA
2 DASHES ANGOSTURA BITTERS
1 DASH ORANGE BITTERS
1 PINCH ACTIVATED CHARCOAL
BRANDY CHERRY (GARNISH)

In a cocktail shaker filled with ice, add the rye whiskey, Averna, both bitters, and activated charcoal. Shake vigorously 8 to 10 times, and strain into a martini glass. Garnish with a brandy cherry.

LATIN CONFUSION
MAKES 1 COCKTAIL (3 OUNCES)

Not long ago, I was working on developing a Latin-inspired pork belly dish. At the time, it seemed every restaurant in the neighborhood was offering smoked pork belly. Nevertheless, I added the components I was working on into the smoker along with some hickory chips and agave syrup. I wish every one of you could have seen the smile on my face when I first tried smoked agave. I started adding the syrup to everything. One day I shared the syrup with the bar manager of a restaurant in Bellevue, Washington, and asked if she could craft a cocktail with smoked agave and bourbon. What she put in front of me that day was nothing short of miraculous. This, in my humble opinion, is the perfect cocktail. Whether it is hot outside, cold, rainy, windy, or rainy, this drink it sure to please.

1½ OUNCES PREMIUM BOURBON

½ OUNCE DRY CURACAO

¼ OUNCE CRÈME DE CACAO

¼ OUNCE SMOKED AGAVE
   (RECIPE FOLLOWS)

3 DASHES CHOCOLATE BITTERS

RIM: 50/50 MIXTURE OF SALT
   AND SUGAR

In a cocktail shaker filled with ice, add the bourbon, dry curacao, crème de cacao, smoked agave, and chocolate bitters. Stir with a bar spoon. Next, rim a rocks glass with a 50/50 mixture of salt and sugar, and fill the glass with ice. Strain the cocktail into the glass and serve.

SMOKED AGAVE
MAKES 1 CUP

---

1 CUP AGAVE

To make the Smoked Agave, preheat smoker to 250°F. Place 1 cup of agave syrup in the smoking tray (or a tray that goes in a smoker) and smoke for 20 minutes. Remove from smoker and allow to cool.

SMOKED DAIQUIRI

MAKES 1 COCKTAIL (3 OUNCES)

The first trip my wife and I ever took together was to Hawaii. Neither of us had never been there before. One afternoon we strolled down to the beach and took refuge from the sweltering sun under a cabana in front of a bar. Katie, without hesitation, ordered a daiquiri. Me, wanting to impress her, as we were still in the early stages of our relationship, asked for the same. We sat there, holding hands with one hand, our daiquiris in the other. Before that trip, I never saw myself as a daiquiri man. Today, I'm proud to say the iconic tropical beverage is one of my favorite cocktails.

---

2 OUNCES PREMIUM WHITE RUM

1 OUNCE LIME JUICE

½ OUNCE SMOKED SIMPLE SYRUP (RECIPE FOLLOWS)

CHARRED LIME WEDGE (GARNISH)

In a cocktail shaker filled with ice, add the rum, lime juice, and Smoked Simple Syrup. Shake vigorously 8 to 10 times, and strain into a coupe glass. Garnish with a charred lime wedge.

SMOKED SIMPLE SYRUP

MAKES 2 CUPS

---

1 CUP WATER

1 CUP SUGAR

Preheat an outdoor smoker to 350°F (page 12).

Place the water and sugar in a pot and bring to a boil. Boil until the sugar has dissolved and the liquid is one homogenous mixture. Remove from heat and transfer to a container that is able to be placed in the smoker.

Smoke the syrup for 30 minutes. Remove from the smoker and let chill. Store in a sealed container in the refrigerator until ready to use. The syrup will stay fresh and flavorful for up to 1 month.

SMOKED OLD FASHIONED
MAKES 1 COCKTAIL [2 ½ OUNCES]

Introducing smoke into your cocktails is a savory change from the mundane of everyday adult beverages. In the restaurant, we keep a bottle of Smoked Simple Syrup on hand so we can tweak any flavor profile at a moment's notice, and so should you. Here's another smoky riff on a classic cocktail.

---

2 OUNCES PREMIUM RYE
WHISKEY
½ OUNCE SMOKED SIMPLE
SYRUP (PAGE 67)
4 DASHES ANGOSTURA BITTERS
ORANGE PEEL (GARNISH)

In a cocktail shaker filled with ice, add the rye whiskey, Smoked Simple Syrup, and bitters. Stir well, and strain into an Old Fashioned glass filled with one large ice cube. Garnish with an orange peel.

SMOKY SAZERAC
MAKES 1 COCKTAIL [2 ½ OUNCES]

The Sazerac is another one of my favorite cocktails. Throughout the years, I have tried many variations, all with their own subtle nuances that makes them unique. This one consistently stands out as a crowd favorite. The smokiness from the mescal offers a whimsical spin on the classic, which is usually made with rye.

---

2 OUNCES PREMIUM REPOSADO
MESCAL
¼ OUNCE AGAVE SYRUP
6 DASHES PEYCHAUDS BITTERS
LEMON PEEL (GARNISH)

In a cocktail shaker filled with ice, add the mescal, agave syrup, and bitters. Shake vigorously 8 to 10 times, and strain into a rocks glass. Garnish with a lemon peel.

ROASTED & SMOKED HORS D'OEUVRES & SMALL BITES

ALBACORE TATAKI | 70

CARAMELIZED BEET BITES WITH WHIPPED CHÉVRE & TOASTED PISTACHIOS | 71

GRILLED ANAHEIM PEPPERS | 73

GRILLED CHICKEN SATAY | 77

GRILLED OYSTERS | 78

ROASTED STUFFED MUSHROOMS | 80

SMOKED BONE MARROW WITH ROASTED CHERRIES | 81

SMOKED DEVILED EGGS | 85

SMOKED FIG WITH FOIE GRAS MOUSSE | 86

LAMB TARTARE WITH SMOKED RADISH GREEN AIOLI | 88

SMOKED RACLETTE FONDUE | 90

SMOKED SALMON "NICOISE" | 91

SMOKED SCALLOP CEVICHE | 92

ALBACORE TATAKI
SERVES 4

The Japanese style of Tataki is a process of quickly searing a fish so the outside is cooked but the inside remains raw, creating almost a shell-like exterior around the fish. In this recipe, I have adapted the Japanese cooking style and added my own twist. First, I crust the albacore with my Latin Rub. This creates a more acidic shell than normal. You can also use salt and pepper if you find the Latin Rub is a little too hot for your palette. You can also experiment with other spice blends or create your own. The key to success with this recipe is ensuring you have a properly heated cast-iron pan. Make sure to get the oil just to the smoke point, but not so hot that you're in danger of lighting the kitchen on fire. Use long tongs, as any moisture that makes its way into the pan will splatter.

½ POUND FRESH ALBACORE LOIN

1 TABLESPOON SESAME OIL

½ CUP LATIN RUB (PAGE 34)

½ CUP CANOLA OIL

1 LIME

2 SCALLIONS, SLICED ON A BIAS

SEA SALT, AS NEEDED

Trim the albacore of any excess bloodline or skin the fishmonger may have left behind. Cut the loin into cubes, about 1½ inches by 1½ inches. Toss the cubes gently with the sesame oil and coat with the Latin Rub.

In a medium-sized heavy-bottomed cast-iron pan, heat the canola oil over medium-high heat. Using tongs, carefully place the albacore cubes in the pan, careful not to overcrowd. Sear in batches, if necessary. Let the albacore sear for 15 seconds on each side. Carefully remove the cubes and transfer to a tray. Place in the refrigerator to immediately cool the fish.

When ready to serve, cut each cube at an angle, from corner to corner. You should be left with a perfect center of raw albacore from each sliced cube. Arrange on a serving tray and garnish with the scallions. Squeeze some lime juice over the top and sprinkle with sea salt.

Note: You can also garnish the dish with shaved radishes, Korean chili threads, or sliced jalapeños. This fish also works atop a Grilled Watermelon Salad (page 166).

CARAMELIZED BEET BITES WITH WHIPPED CHÈVRE & TOASTED PISTACHIOS

MAKES 32 BITES

One of my favorite passions about being a professional chef is the ability to introduce people to foods that are familiar to them but with a whimsical twist. This hors d'oeuvre is a great representation of that twist—a classical dish prepared in a progressive preparation. Beets and goat cheese are a timeless classic often served at buffets and other large gatherings.
Introducing a high-heat method for caramelizing the beets alters the flavor in a truly elevating and savory way while adding yet another level of delicious texture.

---

5 POUNDS RED OR GOLDEN BEETS

2 LARGE ONIONS, ROUGHLY CHOPPED

1 LARGE CARROT, PEELED AND ROUGHLY CHOP

½ CUP BLACK PEPPERCORNS

¼ CUP WHOLE CORIANDER

½ CUP OLIVE OIL

½ CUP SALT

COLD WATER, AS NEEDED

CANOLA OIL, FOR SAUTÉING, AS NEEDED

WHIPPED CHÉVRE (RECIPE FOLLOWS)

TOASTED PISTACHIOS (RECIPE FOLLOWS)

Trim the tops and bottoms off the beets. Using a large stock pot, add the beets along with the onions, carrot, peppercorns, coriander, olive oil, and salt. Then add enough water so the water level reaches a few inches above the beets. Bring to a boil over high heat, then reduce to a simmer. Depending on the size of the beets, cooking time will vary. Average time is about 45 minutes. After 30 minutes, prod the largest beet to its center using either a small knife or a skewer. The beet should offer minimal resistance. Once completely cooked, remove from braising liquid and let cool completely.

Once cooled, peel away the skins of the beets with a vegetable peeler. Using a cutting board and a sharp knife, carefully cut the beets into bite-sized pieces, about 1-inch cubes.

Using a large sauté pan, coat the bottom with canola oil and place over medium-high heat. When hot, caramelize the beets by sautéing them 1 or 2 cups at a time. Set aside and let cool.

To assemble, place the beets on a serving platter. Pipe (or spoon) a small amount of Whipped Chèvre onto the top of the beets and garnish with the Toasted Pistachios.

WHIPPED CHÈVRE

2 CUPS PASTEURIZED GOAT
  CHEESE

¼ CUP BUTTERMILK

ZEST FROM 1 LIME

1 TEASPOON KOSHER SALT

1 TABLESPOON MINCED
  TARRAGON LEAVES

1 TABLESPOON MINCED FLAT-
  LEAF PARSLEY LEAVES

1 TABLESPOON MINCED CHIVES

Using a kitchen or standing mixer, add the goat cheese (the chèvre) and buttermilk. Using the whisk attachment, set on low and whip for 1 minute. Raise the speed to medium-high and whip for 1 additional minute. Turn off the mixer and add the lime zest, salt, tarragon, parsley, and chives. Turn the mixer back on and whip on high speed for 15 seconds or until all the ingredients are thoroughly mixed. If you have piping bags available to you, this would be the time to transfer the mixture to a piping bag. If not, simply transfer the mixture to a clean container until ready to use.

TOASTED PISTACHIOS

1 CUP PISTACHIOS, SHELLED

1 TEASPOON KOSHER SALT

1 TEASPOON ALEPPO POWDER
  OR CHILI POWDER

1 TEASPOON GROUND
  CORIANDER

2 TABLESPOONS OLIVE OIL

Preheat an oven or outdoor grill to 350°F.

In a bowl, add the pistachios, salt, Aleppo, ground coriander, and olive oil. Mix thoroughly. Place the mixture on a sheet pan and toast in the oven or outdoor grill for 4 minutes. Rotate the pan 180 degrees and toast for an additional 4 minutes. Remove from the oven and let cool. Once cool enough to work with, place the pistachios on a cutting board and roughly chop the nuts to break them into smaller pieces. Set aside.

GRILLED ANAHEIM PEPPERS
SERVES 4 (2 PEPPERS PER PERSON)

To me, fresh peppers mean summer is here and backyard barbecue season is upon us! For several months of the year in the Pacific Northwest, my friends and I hang out in the backyard and indulge in mindless banter, microbrews, and grilled meats. Within my group of friends, there's the constant struggle to impress, as their expectations are higher than what you would expect from a typical backyard barbecue. Every year, the bar seems to get higher. As a chef who likes a constant challenge, I never shy away from trying to meet expectations. Without question, grilling and stuffing peppers is always fun, and they always turn out delicious. For a whimsical twist, I like to stuff my peppers with an herb-cheese blend and wrap them in prosciutto. Feel free to play with other ingredients and find a combination that works well for you and those you are entertaining.

---

8 ANAHEIM PEPPERS

CANOLA OIL, AS NEEDED, DIVIDED

2 GARLIC CLOVES, MINCED

½ CUP DICED YELLOW ONION

¼ CUP WHITE WINE

6 OUNCES CHÉVRE

2 TABLESPOONS MINCED THYME LEAVES

1 TABLESPOON MINCED ROSEMARY

1 TABLESPOON MINCED CHIVES

1 TABLESPOON MINCED FLAT-LEAF PARSLEY

1 TEASPOON KOSHER SALT

1 TEASPOON FRESH CRACKED BLACK PEPPER

8 LARGE SLICES PROSCIUTTO

Preheat an outdoor grill (page 10)

Toss the peppers in just enough oil to lightly coat. Place the peppers on the grill and allow to slightly char on all sides until they begin to bubble. Remove from the grill and place in a bowl. Cover tightly with plastic wrap or foil, and let sit for 30 minutes.

Remove the peppers from the bowl, and under running water, gently peel away the skins from the peppers. Using a sharp knife, make a slit on one side of the pepper, just enough to remove the seeds. (Note: the larger the slit in the pepper, the easier they will be to stuff, but the harder it will be to keep them together during the grilling process.) Set the peppers aside.

Bring a sauté pan up to medium-high heat, and add about 2 tablespoons of canola oil. Add the garlic and onions and allow to sweat for 5 minutes. Deglaze the pan by adding the wine, and continue to cook until all the wine has evaporated. Remove from heat.

(Recipe continues on page 76)

In a mixing bowl, using the whisk attachment set on high, whip the chévre for 3 minutes to aerate. Turn off the mixer and add the onions, thyme, rosemary, chives, parsley, and salt and pepper. Continue to whisk on high for 2 additional minutes. Using a small spoon, fill the peppers to capacity with the mixture. Once filled, lay the prosciutto flat and place a stuffed pepper on top. Roll the prosciutto around the pepper tightly. Repeat with all the peppers. Place the rolled peppers on the preheated grill, with the seam of the prosciutto down to create a seal. Then roast on all sides for about 2 minutes each.

Remove from heat and serve immediately.

GRILLED CHICKEN SATAY
SERVES 8 (2 PER PERSON)

Chicken is both elegant and complex, so I have no qualms about serving chicken at a dinner party. Chicken is also very approachable, especially for kids. Satay, as it relates to this recipe, is a popular street food in southeast Asia, mainly Indonesia, consisting of marinated meat grilled over an open flame. Many southeast Asian cultures have their own variation of Satay. In Malaysia particularly, Satay is prominent from quiet street corners to bustling high-end restaurants and everything in between.

¼ CUP GRAPESEED OR CANOLA OIL

3 GARLIC CLOVES, PEELED

1 YELLOW ONION, PEELED AND ROUGHLY CHOPPED

1 TEASPOON GINGER POWDER

1 TEASPOON ALEPPO POWDER OR CHILI POWDER

1 TABLESPOON TURMERIC POWDER

¼ CUP CHOPPED LEMONGRASS (WHITE PART ONLY)

¼ CUP CHOPPED CILANTRO

1 TABLESPOON HONEY

COLD WATER, IF NECESSARY

4 BONELESS SKINLESS CHICKEN BREASTS

16 BAMBOO SKEWERS (PRESOAKED IN COLD WATER FOR AT LEAST 1 HOUR)

Make the marinade by adding the oil, garlic, onion, ginger, Aleppo and turmeric powders, lemongrass, cilantro, and honey into a kitchen or stand-up blender. (Note: You may need to add a little cold water to help combine the mixture, depending on the equipment you are using.) Using a sharp knife, cut each chicken breast into 4 equal-sized pieces. Place the chicken in the marinade and let sit in the refrigerator at least 2 hours, up to 24 hours.

Preheat an outdoor grill (page 10).

Skewer the marinated chicken onto the presoaked bamboo skewers. Place the skewers on the grill, perpendicular to the grates, one at a time. Allow to cook 2 minutes and caramelize on each side before turning. Serve as is, or with a side of your favorite peanut sauce.

GRILLED OYSTERS
SERVES 4 (3 OYSTERS PER PERSON)

Love them or hate them, oysters are an international superstar. They are ocean candy wrapped in a beautiful porcelain shell. They represent class and prestige and signify wealth and success. No wonder oysters are at the top of the list for those trying to impress. Oysters have been cultivated for thousands of years and have undergone multiple identities over generations. During the nineteenth century, oysters were in abundance and were inexpensive food for the working class. Today, oysters are reserved not only for the upper echelon of society, but also for the masses. They are no longer found in only the highest tiered restaurants, but rather in grocery stores, farmers' markets, and many dining establishments around America. When I hear someone say, "I don't like oysters," my reply is always the same: "It's because you haven't had a good oyster." Oysters are extremely versatile. You can smoke, bake, fry, grill, or sauté them. My two favorite recipes? The first: simply grill them until they open, hit them with a shot of lime juice and some sea salt, and slurp away. The second is this savory recipe for baking them.

---

1 BUNCH WATERCRESS

2 TABLESPOONS UNSALTED
   BUTTER

2 CLOVES GARLIC, SMASHED

1 MINCED SHALLOT

⅔ CUP MAYONNAISE OR AIOLI

1 TABLESPOON MINCED CAPERS

3 OUNCES PARMESAN CHEESE
   (OR COMPARABLE CHEESE)

1 TABLESPOON LIME JUICE

1 TABLESPOON COGNAC

1 TEASPOON SALT AND PEPPER
   MIX (50/50 BLEND)

12 MEDIUM TO LARGE OYSTERS,
   SHUCKED

Preheat the oven or outdoor grill to 400°F.

Remove the stems from the watercress. In a small pot, melt the butter over low heat, and add the garlic and shallot. Sweat over medium-low heat until the shallots are translucent. Remove from the heat and add the watercress, stirring constantly until the leaves are wilted, about 30 seconds. Using a food processor or blender, add the mayonnaise, capers, cheese, lime juice, and cognac, and pulse for 1 minute, until smooth. Add the melted butter mix, salt mix, and pulse for an additional 10 seconds.

Place the oysters on a tray for grilling or roasting, and place a teaspoon to tablespoon size of the mix over each oyster, enough to cover the entire surface of the open-faced oyster. If you are using an oven, place on the middle rack and roast for 8 to 10 minutes. If you are using an outdoor grill, place the oysters either directly on the grill or use a tray to set them inside the grill, and roast for 10 minutes.

Remove from the heat and serve immediately.

ROASTED STUFFED MUSHROOMS
SERVES 8 (3 PER PERSON)

When you think of stuffed mushrooms, you may think of an appetizer straight out of a 1978 issue of *Good Housekeeping*, but that's okay. This is an hors d'oeuvre every home cook should have in their arsenal. This is because they are delicious, relatively inexpensive, and pretty darn easy to make. With stuffed mushrooms, it's more about technique and procedure than the actual recipe. Yes, there are hundreds, if not thousands, of stuffed mushroom recipes, all claiming to be the best. Ultimately, the best is going to be the mushrooms you make yourself.

---

24 BUTTON MUSHROOMS

1 LARGE YELLOW ONION, PEELED AND SMALL DICE

2 GARLIC CLOVES, PEELED AND MINCED

3 OUNCES UNSALTED BUTTER

1 TABLESPOON KOSHER SALT

1½ TEASPOONS FRESH GROUND BLACK PEPPER

½ CUP WHITE WINE

2 TABLESPOONS MINCED THYME LEAVES

1 TEASPOON CAYENNE PEPPER

½ CUP PANKO BREAD CRUMBS

1 CUP GRATED PARMESAN CHEESE + ½ CUP

1 LARGE EGG

Clean the mushrooms by simply submerging them in water and agitating the water with your fingers like a washing machine. Remove the mushrooms and place on a towel to dry. Remove the stems and place the mushroom stems in a kitchen or stand-up blender Add the onion and garlic. Pulse the stem mixture until the pieces are about the size of a grain of rice.

Preheat a large sauté pan over medium-high heat and add the butter. Allow the butter to melt and slightly brown. Add the stem mixture to the pan. Add the salt and pepper and stir constantly for 5 minutes. Add the white wine and continue cooking until the liquid has evaporated. Add the thyme leaves and cayenne pepper. Stir and remove from heat. Allow the mixture to cool at least 10 minutes. Meanwhile, place the mushrooms caps on a roasting tray, cap-side up.

Preheat oven to 350°F.

And the panko and Parmesan cheese to the cooled mixture and mix well. Before adding the raw egg, taste and adjust the mixture to your liking, if necessary. Add the egg and mix well again. Using a small spoon, fill the mushroom cups with the mixture. Sprinkle the rest of the Parmesan cheese over each individual mushroom cap. Roast the caps for 20 minutes, or until the tops are golden brown.

Remove from heat and serve.

SMOKED BONE MARROW WITH ROASTED CHERRIES
SERVES 8 (1 BONE PER PERSON)

As a chef, one of the questions I'm commonly asked is, "Can you remember your favorite bite of food?" My answer is, "Yes, Smoked Bone Marrow with Roasted Cherries." I remember that first bite like it was yesterday. It had everything you could ever want out of a perfect meal, in one bite. The richness and umami of the marrow, the smokiness from the cooking process, the crunch from the brioche it was served on, the sweet and tangy tartness from the cherries, the allium from the shallots, and the earthiness from the herbs. Roasted bone marrow has been a staple on my menus for the last ten years, as it serves two purposes. The first is to get my guests to try something they would not normally experience. Second, it's delicious. A trip to your local butcher should help you obtain the perfect marrow bones for this appetizer. The butcher may ask how you would like the bones cut. You will want them canoed (think of the shape of a canoe). This will allow for easiest access to the marrow inside while giving more surface area to absorb the smoke.

---

8 CANOED PIPE BONES

ALL-PURPOSE BRINE (RECIPE FOLLOWS)

1 CUP FRESH SEASONAL CHERRIES (RAINIER OR BING)

1 TEASPOON EXTRA-VIRGIN OLIVE OIL

1 TEASPOON LIME JUICE, OR TO TASTE

2 TABLESPOONS MINCED SHALLOTS

¼ CUP FLAT-LEAF PARSLEY LEAVES

½ CUP CRUMBLED FETA CHEESE

Place the bones in a suitable container, and pour the brine over the bones. Let sit in the refrigerator overnight. (Note: You can skip this step, but I recommend you brine the bones to help draw out some of the blood.)

Preheat an outdoor smoker to 175°F.

Place the bones with the marrow facing up on a smoking tray and smoke for 1 hour. If your smoker does not have a heat setting, only smoke for 20 minutes, as the bones tend to smoke hotter and you don't want the marrow melting away (remember marrow reacts like butter).

Meanwhile, preheat the oven to 400°F.

(Recipe continues on page 83)

Halve the cherries and remove the seeds. Toss the cherries with the olive oil, then salt and arrange on a parchment-lined roasting tray. Roast in the oven for 15 minutes. When the cherries are soft, remove from oven and allow to cool. In a mixing bowl, mix the cherries with the lime juice, shallots, parsley, and feta.

Remove the bones from the smoker. At this point, you can either immediately place the bones in the oven or allow them to cool to roast later. (Note: The bones must stay refrigerated if you are going to roast them later.) Roast the bones in the oven for 10 minutes, or 14 minutes in a conventional oven. Remove from oven and place on a serving tray. Assemble the cherry mixture over the top of the bones and serve with sliced bread or crackers.

ALL PURPOSE BRINE
MAKES 5 QUARTS

Brining, a flavored saline solution used to flavor and oversaturate meats, is often an overlooked step when cooking. Because of the high salinity of the brine, meats will absorb the liquid, which then sacrifices itself to the heat, leaving behind the natural juices while not drying out the protein. In the restaurant, we always keep on hand a large batch of what we call "All Purpose Brine." Although a basic brine is made up of 1 cup of salt to 1 gallon of water, this recipe calls for different floral notes like oranges and limes.

1 GALLON WATER

1 CUP KOSHER SALT

¼ CUP SUGAR

1 ORANGE HALVED

2 LIMES HALVED

1 LEMON HALVED

¼ CUP PEPPERCORNS

6 GARLIC CLOVES PEELED

1 BUNCH THYME

In a large pot, add the water, salt, sugar, orange, limes, lemon, peppercorns, cloves, and thyme. Bring to a boil over high heat. Continue to boil until the salt and sugar are dissolved, about 5 minutes. Remove from heat and allow to cool. Do not strain. Notes: If not using the brine right away, store in a sealed container in the refrigerator up to 2 weeks. Only use the brine once when brining meat, then discard.

SMOKED DEVILED EGGS
SERVES 12 (2 HALVES PER PERSON)

Ever wonder why they're called *deviled* eggs? The term *deviled* was first used in the eighteenth century in reference to any food that was either zesty or spicy. Believe it or not, this picnic favorite has roots that go back to Roman times when nobles would have boiled eggs stuffed with sausage as an appetizer to meals.

The deviled egg, as we know it, didn't evolve to its current state until about the nineteenth century. If you're as lucky as I am, you too have cherished memories of your grandmother making you deviled eggs after school. If you search for recipes, you are sure to be overwhelmed by the sheer volume of different versions. My theory is deviled eggs are like wine—you like what you like. Some include horseradish, stone ground mustard, Sriracha, and so on. When it comes down to it, the deviled eggs you decide to make and serve are going to be the eggs that best represent you. It wasn't long ago when I had the crazy idea to smoke the yolks. The smoky result of cooked yolk, accompanied by the mustard and scallions, created such a flavorful combination I felt it was worthy of a recipe.

---

12 LARGE FARM-FRESH EGGS

COLD WATER, AS NEEDED

¾ CUP MAYONNAISE

1 TABLESPOON STONE GROUND
    MUSTARD

2 TABLESPOONS MINCED
    TARRAGON

1 TABLESPOON MINCED CHIVES

1 TEASPOON KOSHER SALT

4 SLICES COOKED AND CHOPPED
    BACON (OPTIONAL)

¼ CUP CHÉVRE (OPTIONAL)

Add the eggs to a pot and cover with cold water. Bring to a boil over high heat. As soon as the eggs start to boil, remove from heat, cover, and let sit for 11 minutes. Immediately remove the eggs from the water and place in an ice bath to stop the cooking process.

Preheat an outdoor smoker to 250°F.

Peel the eggs, cut them in half, and carefully remove the yolks, setting the whites aside. Smoke the yolks in the smoker for 15 minutes. Remove the yolks from the smoker and transfer to a mixing bowl. Add the mayonnaise, mustard, tarragon, chives, and salt. Add the bacon and chévre, if desired. Mix well to combine.

Use a small spoon to scoop the mixture back into the whites, and serve.

SMOKED FIG WITH FOIE GRAS MOUSSE
SERVES 12 (2 PER PERSON)

As someone who frequently cooks at home for my wife and friends, sometimes we are left wanting to make a great impression while exerting minimal effort due to our busy lives. This foie gras recipe is an outstanding way to fulfill both. Foie gras, if you're not familiar, can be a point of contention in the real world, but in professional kitchens, its uses are abundant. Don't be afraid to experiment with this wonderful product. Smoking the figs, meanwhile, helps develop not only another layer of flavor, but also another layer of texture. Through the smoking process, a small amount of the fig juice is released, tightening the skin and giving the fig a jerky-like texture. Serve these small bites with some chilled champagne and your friends will be inviting themselves back in no time.

---

12 RIPE FIGS

SALT, AS NEEDED

SUGAR, AS NEEDED

½ POUND FOIE GRAS

1 OUNCE COGNAC

½ CUP HEAVY CREAM

½ CUP ALMONDS

CANOLA OIL, AS NEEDED

SALT AND PEPPER, AS NEEDED

Preheat an outdoor smoker (page 12).

Remove the stems from the figs, and slice them in half. Toss them in a bowl with enough oil, salt, and sugar to lightly coat. Smoke the figs using a hard smoke for 10 minutes, then set aside.

Preheat the oven to 350°F.

Add the foie gras to a food processor and blend until the texture is nice and silky. While the food processor is still on, add the cognac and heavy cream until the texture returns to being smooth and silky. Taste and season with additional salt, if necessary.

Toss the almonds in a bowl with some canola oil, salt, and pepper to lightly coat. Arrange the almonds on a sheet tray and roast in the oven for 6 minutes, or until golden brown. Remove from oven and let cool. Once cool, crush the almonds to about the size of rice.

Pipe the foie gras mousse into the smoked fig base, and garnish with the toasted almonds. Sprinkle with salt just before serving.

LAMB TARTARE
WITH SMOKED RADISH GREEN AIOLI
SERVES 4

If you find yourself hosting some adventurous guests, this dish is a must. This whimsical play on the traditional beef tartare will push the boundary of the culinary palate. The sweetness from the lamb, combined with the heat from the pepper, the creaminess from the dressing, and the crunch from the pork rinds is truly an experience. This recipe, incidentally, developed one evening when Ryuji, one of my cooks, brought in a bag of pork rinds. Honestly, I hadn't remembered eating these since I was a kid, so I grabbed a handful. Coincidentally, at the same time, another cook was preparing a beef tartare dish. I grabbed a bite with a pork rind, and a new dish was born. On a personal note, this are how many dishes are born in the restaurant; recipes often come to fruition by serendipitous accidents.

---

1 RACK AMERICAN LAMB

½ CUP KETCHUP

1 TABLESPOON SRIRACHA

1 LIME, ZESTED AND JUICED

1 TEASPOON AGAVE SYRUP

1 TEASPOON CHOPPED
  CILANTRO

1 POBLANO PEPPER, SEEDED
  AND DICED

PINCH OF SALT AND PEPPER

SMOKED RADISH GREEN AIOLI
  (GARNISH, PAGE 56)

1 BAG PLAIN STYLE PORK RINDS

SEA SALT, AS NEEDED

FRESH FLAT-LEAF PARSLEY,
  CHOPPED (FOR GARNISH,
  OPTIONAL)

Remove the lamb from the bone and remove all the silver skin. Cut the loin into long ¼-inch strips, then into ¼-inch strips again. Then dice the strips so you are left with ¼-inch cubes.

In a mixing bowl, add the ketchup, Sriracha, lime zest and juice, agave syrup, cilantro, Poblano pepper, salt, and pepper. Mix well. Add the chopped lamb and toss well. Season to desired taste.

To serve, arrange some pork rinds on a serving platter accompanied by the Lamb Tartare. Garnish with a small amount of Smoked Radish Green Aioli. Finish with a sprinkle of sea salt and some fresh herbs, like flat-leaf parsley.

SMOKED RACLETTE FONDUE
SERVES 8

Raclette is a semi-hard cows' milk cheese from Switzerland that is heated over an open flame to slightly melt and then scraped over a dish. I assure you, it's as delicious as it sounds. Smoking cheese, meanwhile, is one of the most delicious techniques you can master. I'm not sure of the last time I had a cheese that wasn't a little more delicious after it was smoked. You just have to be careful not to over-smoke, because that can make the cheese go downhill in taste real fast. Fondue is equally delicious. As a chef, I am always looking for ways to improve a dish, add depth of flavor, and introduce my dining guests to new experiences. Manipulating the cheese in a way that might not be expected is an excellent way of achieving culinary success. Fondue, incidentally, is unique to this book in that it is one of the few foods that cannot, or rather should not, be eaten on its own. Like most melted cheeses, fondue is best enjoyed with a bevy of breads, fruits, vegetables, and meats. Raclette may not be available in every grocery store, but it is readily available online. If you cannot find raclette locally, you can substitute for gruyere, fontina, or tallegio, to name a few.

---

1 POUND RACLETTE

2 TEASPOONS CORNSTARCH

⅓ CUP WHITE WINE

½ CUP HEAVY CREAM

1 TABLESPOON KOSHER SALT

Preheat an outdoor smoker to 200°F (page 12).

Shred the raclette using a cheese grater and lay out flat onto a tray for smoking. Smoke the cheese for 20 minutes, then carefully remove from smoker. Sprinkle the cornstarch over the top of the cheese and set aside.

Using a heavy-bottom saucepot, bring the wine and cream to a simmer over low heat. Add a small handful of the smoked cheese to the hot liquid, and stir with a whisk, making sure not to add more cheese until the prior addition has melted. Once you have added all the cheese, add the salt. At this point, you can either leave the fondue as is or garnish with some fresh herbs. Serve this fondue with an assortment of crackers, Belgian endive, crostinis, and sliced apples.

SMOKED SALMON "NICOISE"
SERVES 8

It seems you can't pass a market in the Pacific Northwest without seeing a sign for some fresh delicacy from the ocean. Crabs, shrimp, prawns, clams, mussels, oysters, squid, halibut, salmon . . . we have it all. We also have a high population of Native Americans who still pride themselves on the age-old tradition of smoking seafood, specifically salmon. All throughout coastal Washington, various tribes have built smokehouses that I can only assume are old. They also use different types of wood, and expose the fish (usually Chinook and Coho) to high heat smoke for a short period of time. While other cultures tend to slow and cold-smoke their fish, this Native American style of smoking fish at high heat seems to give the fish a deeper and more unique, intense flavor.

---

2 POUNDS FRESH WILD ALASKAN OR PACIFIC SALMON

1 CUP BROWN SUGAR

1 TABLESPOON KOSHER SALT

1 TABLESPOON GROUND CORIANDER

1 TEASPOON GROUND CUMIN

1 TEASPOON FRESH GROUND BLACK PEPPER

½ CUP PREMIUM TEQUILA (OR VODKA OR GIN)

In a bowl, add the brown sugar, salt, coriander, cumin, and pepper. Mix well. Spread a 2-foot-long piece of plastic wrap on a flat surface, and sprinkle the spice mixture evenly in a single layer on the first 8 inches of the plastic, leaving the first 2 inches of the plastic clean. Lay your fillet or pieces of salmon on top of the spice mixture. Sprinkle the remaining mixture over the top, covering all the salmon. Next, gently splash the tequila (or other spirit) over the salmon. Carefully use the excess plastic wrap to completely wrap the salmon. Don't worry if part of the fish is uncovered; as the mix liquefies and settles, it will coat everything. Place the fish in the refrigerator and let sit overnight (Note: To be safe, you may want to set the salmon on a large plate or platter to catch any drippings that might leak from the plastic wrap.)

After at least 12 hours, carefully remove the salmon from the plastic, and gently rinse the fish under cold water to remove all the spices.

Preheat an outdoor smoker to 160°F (page 12).

Pat the salmon dry and lay the fish flat on a smoking tray. Place the salmon in the smoker and let smoke for 1 hour. Remove the fish from the smoker and place in a preheated 350°F oven for 8 minutes. Take out of the oven and let cool.

This smoked salmon works well crumbled over a salad, mixed into scrambled eggs, or tossed with some aioli to make a smoked salmon sandwich. Once you learn the technique behind smoking your own fish, the possibilities seem endless.

SMOKED SCALLOP CEVICHE
SERVES 4

Ceviche is a dish commonly found in Latin American countries, mainly along the coastlines. Submerging seafood in a marinade of citric acid, usually citric juice from lemons or limes, will cause the fish to "cook" the same way heat would. There are two key elements to executing a great ceviche. The first is to buy the freshest seafood available to you. This is a case where you cannot hide a subpar product behind cooking it to death, as any novice eater will see right through it. The second is to have a well-balanced marinade. If your citric acid marinade is too acidic (sour), too sweet, or too salty, it will throw off the entire chemistry of the dish. Smoking seafood for ceviche is not a common practice in the traditional sense, but one that I have found creates another level of satisfying flavor to an already stellar dish. In this recipe, I smoke the scallops prior to cooking, but you can also grill or sear the scallops to create a unique flavor profile. You can also use this recipe for other seafood proteins like prawns, rockfish, or lobster.

---

1 POUND FRESH BAY SCALLOPS
    OR 10–20 DRY-PACK SEA
    SCALLOPS

1 JALAPEÑO, SEEDED AND SMALL
    DICE

½ CUP CHOPPED CILANTRO

2 ROMA TOMATOES, SEEDED
    AND MEDIUM DICE

½ CUP LIME JUICE

½ CUP LEMON JUICE

ZEST FROM 1 LIME

1 TEASPOON GROUND
    CORIANDER

½ SHAVED RED ONION

1 TEASPOON SUGAR

1 TABLESPOON KOSHER SALT

Preheat an outdoor smoker to 350°F (page 12).

Place the scallops on a tray and smoke for 12 minutes. While the scallops are smoking, add the remaining ingredients to a bowl. Mix well.

If using bay scallops, transfer the smoked scallops into the mixture. If you're using the larger sea scallops, quarter the scallops and add to the mixture. Cover tightly and refrigerate. Allow to sit at least 4 hours with a maximum of 24 hours before serving.

Just before serving, gently re-toss the ceviche and taste again—the salinity may have changed as the flavors married. Serve in a chilled bowl along with some crackers or tortilla chips.

CARAMELIZED SOUPS & SALADS

BLACKENED CARROT SALAD | 95

BLACKENED CHICKEN SALAD | 96

CARAMELIZED CARROT SOUP WITH SOUR
CREAM & WALNUTS | 97

CHARRED BROCCOLINI WITH BURNT LIME DRESSING | 100

CHARRED CAULIFLOWER WITH BURNT HONEY DRESSING | 102

CHARRED EGGPLANT SOUP | 103

GRILLED CAESAR SALAD WITH ANCHOVY DRESSING &
SOFT-POACHED EGG | 104

GRILLED FRISÉE WITH BACON VINAIGRETTE | 107

GRILLED TOMATOES WITH BASIL EMULSION | 108

SMOKED CORN CHOWDER | 110

SMOKED CORN | 110

SMOKED POTATO SALAD | 112

BLACKENED CARROT SALAD
SERVES 4

Blackening is an art I consider to be drastically underutilized. When executed properly, a high-heat char can add an additional depth of flavor that is new to most people. Can you remember the last time you went out to eat and was presented with a side dish that had been intentionally blackened? More than likely, no, you can't. A cook, whether at home or in the industry, must be extremely confident in their abilities to present a food to their guests that has been intentionally burned. But that should in no way deter you from making an effort. Practice, fail, practice, and fail again. Eventually, these techniques will become second nature and you will have yet another weapon in your cooking arsenal.

---

6 LARGE CARROTS

½ CUP OLIVE OIL, DIVIDED

¼ CUP CHOPPED CILANTRO

¼ CUP CHOPPED MINT

1 TABLESPOON MINCED CHIVES

1 TABLESPOON LEMON OR LIME JUICE

½ CUP TOASTED PISTACHIOS, CRUSHED

½ TABLESPOON SALT

½ TABLESPOON BLACK PEPPER

¼ CUP FETA CHEESE

Preheat an outdoor grill (page 10).

Peel the carrots and trim the tops. Coat the carrots with ¼ cup olive oil and shake off excess. Place on the grill and allow to char, rolling the carrots every few minutes to burn evenly. Once charred, remove the carrots from the grill and place in a covered container. Allow to steam for 20 minutes. Once cool, place on a cutting board, and cut the carrots into 1-inch-long pieces, rolling the carrots a half turn after every cut so that each piece is cut uniquely. Transfer the carrots to a bowl, and add the cilantro, mint, chives, lemon or lime juice, crushed pistachios, and salt and pepper, adjusting the seasoning to your taste. Place in serving bowl and garnish with the feta cheese.

BLACKENED CHICKEN SALAD
SERVES 4

Popularized by chef Paul Prudhomme, a Louisiana native, the art of properly blackening proteins is not easily mastered. Over the course of one's culinary career, pans are ruined and proteins are annihilated by chefs trying to bring a little flare to their cuisine. The most important element to consider when blackening foods is to be careful! Of course, have fun with this cooking technique, but definitely watch the temperature of your pan. Chicken breasts are notorious for overcooking and they can get away from you in a hurry. There's nothing worse than taking the time to be meticulous with your measuring and procedure only to end up with dry chicken. I recommend taking the extra time to brine the chicken before starting the blackening process.

4 BONELESS SKINLESS CHICKEN
    BREASTS
½ CUP BLACKENING SPICE
    (PAGE 30)
1 CUP CANOLA OIL
SPRING MIX, AS NEEDED
DRESSING OF CHOICE, AS
    NEEDED

Preheat the oven to 400˚F.

Generously coat the chicken breasts with the Blackening Spice and set on a parchment-lined baking sheet.

Coat the bottom of a cast-iron skillet with the canola oil and heat. When hot, gently lay the chicken breasts, one at a time, in the pan and allow them to blacken, about 1 minute. Turn over and allow the other side to blacken. Remove the blackened chicken from the skillet and transfer back to the baking sheet. Place in oven for 5 to 7 minutes, or until the internal temperature of the chicken reaches 165˚F.

Set the chicken aside and place a sheet of aluminum foil gently over the breasts to allow the juices to relax back into the meat.

Toss a fresh spring mix with your favorite salad dressing. This blackened chicken goes well with many dressings, from bleu cheese, to ranch, to vinaigrettes, and everything in between. Carefully slice the chicken into pieces about the width of your thumb, and place on top of the salad and serve.

CARAMELIZED CARROT SOUP
WITH SOUR CREAM & WALNUTS
SERVES 12

I didn't find true appreciation for a well-crafted soup until later in life. Many consider soup an afterthought, a superfluous necessity. Students in the professional culinary arts are a bit stunned to discover that when they stage in a traditional French kitchen, one of their tests is to create a soup. But for those who are experienced, assembling a soup is a true display of one's skill and resources. Some years ago, I worked for a chef who taught me a valuable lesson I still preach to this day: "You cannot make flavor in a pan." And he's right, which makes me think about every ingredient I put into every dish, particularly when it comes to soups. Should I add water? How about chicken stock instead? Should I make carrot soup? What if I caramelized the carrots first? Would caramelized carrots further enhance the flavor? You should not wait until the end of the cooking process to decide what a soup needs, as many people do. Instead, start at the beginning, like I do with this delicious recipe. This soup is a great winter dish that I serve to family and friends before the holiday meal.

---

3 POUNDS CARROTS

½ CUP CANOLA OIL

1 TABLESPOON SALT

2 OUNCES UNSALTED BUTTER

½ CUP YELLOW OR WHITE ONION, PEELED AND CHOPPED

3 GLOVES GARLIC, PEELED AND MINCED

½ CUP WHITE WINE

1 TEASPOON GROUND CORIANDER

1 TEASPOON GROUND CUMIN

6 CUPS CHICKEN OR VEGETABLE STOCK

1 LIME, ZESTED AND JUICED

Preheat the oven to 400°F.

Peel and chop carrots into ½-inch pieces. Add the carrots to a bowl with the oil and salt. Toss well, then arrange the carrots in one layer on a roasting sheet. Roast for 20 to 25 minutes until carrots start to caramelize. At the 20-minute mark, poke one of the carrots in the middle of the tray with a knife; there shouldn't be any resistance. If there is, keep roasting until there isn't any. Remove from the oven and set aside.

In a large pot, melt the butter over medium heat, and add the onions and garlic. Sweat for 5 minutes. When the onions are translucent, deglaze with the wine and allow the wine to evaporate. Then add the carrots, coriander, and cumin and cook for another 5 minutes over medium heat, stirring almost constantly so the carrots don't burn.

(Recipe continues on page 98)

½ CUP SOUR CREAM

½ CUP MINCED CHIVES OR
   PARSLEY

1 CUP WALNUTS, ROASTED AND
   CHOPPED

Add the stock, lime zest and juice, and bring to a boil, then reduce to a simmer on low heat. Simmer for 20 minutes, then remove from the heat. There are two methods for the next process using either an immersion blender or kitchen blender.

Immersion blender: Add the sour cream and blend on high until a smooth purée-like consistency. Kitchen blender: Wait until the soup is cool (under 70°F), and working in small batches, purée the soup adding a little of the sour cream at a time until you have blended the entire mixture.

Using a chinois, strain the soup and season to taste. This soup is great served hot or cold. To serve, garnish with the chives or parsley and walnuts.

CHARRED BROCCOLINI WITH BURNT LIME DRESSING

SERVES 4

This fantastic and simple dish is great for any occasion, whether a backyard barbecue or Sunday family meal. My grandmother served this dish as a salad at the picnics she would have in her backyard. You can serve it warm or at room temperature. The recipe calls for broccolini, but you can easily interchange the vegetable for green beans, cauliflower, or asparagus. Don't be afraid to swap out the garnishes, too. Find something fresh that you like and experiment with it. The mint and lime I suggest for the garnish will give this dish an almost mojito-like quality; however, you can also garnish with cilantro, parsley, chives, shredded cheese, virtually any nut, even croutons.

1 POUND BROCCOLINI

2 LIMES

½ CUP NEUTRAL OIL (CANOLA)

1 MEDIUM SHALLOT, PEELED
    AND MINCED

1 TEASPOON COURSE SEA SALT

TOASTED PISTACHIOS AND
    FRESH MINT (GARNISH,
    OPTIONAL)

Bring a large pot of heavily salted water to a boil. Next, prepare an ice bath.

Remove 1 to 1½ inches off the bottom of the broccolini. (Note: the bottom is usually dry and not as palatable.) When the water is at a rolling boil, drop half of the broccolini into the water for 30 seconds, then immediately remove and place in the ice bath. Repeat the process with the remaining broccolini. When the broccolini have cooled, remove from the ice bath, pat dry, and set aside.

Preheat an outdoor grill (page 12).

Using a zester or microplane, zest both limes, reserving the zest. Next, cut both limes in half and place the halves on the grill to char. Depending on the type and heat of your grill, times will vary, but it shouldn't take more than 5 minutes for a good char.

Remove the limes from the grill and squeeze the juice into a small mixing bowl. Add the oil, zest, shallot, and salt and mix to combine. Set the Burnt Lime Dressing aside.

Arrange the broccolini in one layer over the grill to caramelize, about 3 minutes on each side, or until nicely charred. Remove from the grill and toss the broccolini with the Burnt Lime Dressing.

To serve, garnish with some toasted pistachios and some fresh mint.

CHARRED CAULIFLOWER WITH BURNT HONEY DRESSING

SERVES 4

In the Skagit Valley, just north of Seattle, is some of the best cauliflower. I've been fortunate enough to visit many of these produce farms and work alongside the farmers. One evening after working at one, a farmer and I lit a fire beside his house to grill some steaks. We had cauliflower left over so I tossed some in olive oil and placed them on the grill. That day forever changed the way I looked at vegetables. Today, I serve this dish as a warm or room-temperature salad at my restaurant. If you don't have an outdoor grill, leave the head whole, coat the entire cauliflower with the oil and seasonings as instructed, and roast in a 450°F oven for about 20 minutes.

1 LARGE OR 2 SMALL HEADS
   CAULIFLOWER
½ CUP EXTRA-VIRGIN OLIVE OIL
2 TABLESPOONS PROVENCAL
   SPICE RUB (PAGE 37)
2 TEASPOONS KOSHER SALT
1 TEASPOON FRESH GROUND
   BLACK PEPPER
BURNT HONEY DRESSING
   (RECIPE FOLLOWS)

Preheat an outdoor grill (page 10).

Slice the cauliflower in long pieces, starting from the outside moving toward the center so that every slice retains a piece of the core. Coat each piece with olive oil, then the Provencal Spice Rub, salt, and pepper. Place each slice on the grill and let char for 4 minutes. Turn over and grill the other side for 4 minutes.

Remove from the grill, toss the cauliflower in a bowl with the Burnt Honey Dressing, and serve.

BURNT HONEY DRESSING

MAKES ¾ CUP

¼ CUP HONEY
1 MEDIUM SHALLOT, PEELED
   AND MINCED
¼ CUP GRAPEFRUIT JUICE
1 TEASPOON STONE GROUND
   MUSTARD
1 TABLESPOON CHAMPAGNE
   VINEGAR
1 TABLESPOON EXTRA-VIRGIN
   OLIVE OIL
SALT AND PEPPER, TO TASTE

In a small sauce pot over medium heat, add the honey and scald it until it just begins to brown. Add the shallot and whisk constantly for 30 seconds. Add the grapefruit juice and continue to whisk until the mixture become homogenous. Add the mustard, vinegar, and olive oil while continuing whisking until homogenous. Remove from the heat and allow to cool. Season with salt and pepper, to taste.

CHARRED EGGPLANT SOUP
SERVES 12

I consider the eggplant a beautiful vegetable. It's the tofu of the solid vegetable world. Eggplant isn't packed with a lot of flavor, but it can be manipulated in almost any form to create fantastic dishes. You can char, smoke, grill, fry, roast, and sauté eggplant. Without question, eggplant can withstand any high-heat method. For this recipe, charring the eggplant thoroughly allows the transformation of the relatively dense meat into a softer consistency that, when puréed into a soup, will add a velvety texture makes cream unnecessary.

2 MEDIUM EGGPLANTS

OLIVE OIL, AS NEEDED

8 OUNCES (2 STICKS) UNSALTED BUTTER

1 POUND ROMA TOMATOES

1 MEDIUM YELLOW ONION, PEELED AND CHOPPED

4 CLOVES GARLIC, PEELED AND MINCED

1 TEASPOON GROUND CUMIN

1 TEASPOON FRESH GROUND BLACK PEPPER

1 TEASPOON CORIANDER

6 CUPS CHICKEN OR VEGETABLE STOCK

½ CUP HEAVY CREAM (OPTIONAL)

Preheat an outdoor grill (page 10). Peel the eggplants and cut into disks about the width of your thumb. Dress both sides generously with olive oil and arrange on a baking sheet. Transfer to the grill and fully char both sides. Depending on the heat of your grill, cooking times will vary. Once charred on both sides, remove the eggplant from the grill and return to the baking sheet. The eggplants should be completely soft.

In a large pot, melt the butter over medium-low heat. Cut the tomatoes into medium-sized pieces (each piece about the size of a marble) and add to the pot along with the onion, garlic, cumin, pepper, and coriander. Sweat the onion for 5 minutes, stirring constantly so nothing burns. Add the stock and bring to a boil, then reduce to a simmer over low heat. Simmer for 20 minutes. Remove from heat. There are two methods for the next process using either an immersion blender or kitchen blender.

Immersion blender: Add the heavy cream and blend on high until a smooth purée-like consistency. Kitchen blender: Wait until the soup is cool (under 70°F), and working in small batches, purée the soup adding a little of the heavy cream at a time until you have blended the entire mixture.

Using a chinois, strain the soup and season to taste. Serve hot. Note: If bringing the soup up from cold, place the soup in a pot over medium heat, and whisk almost constantly until hot.

GRILLED CAESAR SALAD WITH ANCHOVY
DRESSING & SOFT-POACHED EGG

SERVES 4

I doubt there's a person in America who has never had a Caesar Salad. Caesars seem to be everywhere, from kits in a bag at the grocery store to assembled table-side at high-end steakhouses. Without question, this surprisingly complex flavored salad isn't going away any time soon, nor should it. The timeless classic has solidified its place in culinary history as one of the greats. More recently, chefs have been offering a twist on the Caesar by grilling the greens. Introducing high heat to an otherwise delicate leafy green transforms the salad into an unexpected pleasant surprise. That's because the heat breaks down the fibers on the outside, and if done right, still leaves you with that familiar crunch. I use traditional romaine hearts, as they are familiar and available year-round at virtually any grocery store. Castelfranco lettuce also works well if you cannot find romaine seasonally at the store or market.

---

4 ROMAINE HEARTS

OLIVE OIL, AS NEEDED

SALT AND PEPPER, AS NEEDED

ANCHOVY DRESSING (RECIPE FOLLOWS)

6 SOFT-POACHED EGGS (GARNISH, RECIPE FOLLOWS)

Preheat an outdoor grill (page 10).

Slice the romaine hearts in half lengthwise. Season with a little olive oil, salt and pepper, and place flat-side down on the grill. Depending on the heat of your grill, after 30 to 45 seconds, rotate the hearts 45 degrees to achieve a diamond pattern on the flat side of the lettuce. Once slightly charred, remove the hearts from the grill and place in a container that can withstand some heat. Cover with plastic or aluminum foil or set in a warm place for 20 minutes. This allows the lettuce to steam and break down. After 20 minutes, remove the hearts from the container and let cool. Once cool, liberally coat the grilled romaine with Anchovy Dressing and garnish with the Soft Poached Eggs.

ANCHOVY DRESSING

MAKES 1 CUP

½ CUP EXTRA-VIRGIN OLIVE OIL

ZEST FROM 2 LIMES

JUICE FROM 1 LIME

6 ANCHOVY FILLETS, RINSED
   AND MINCED

1 LARGE SHALLOT, PEELED AND
   MINCED

2 TABLESPOONS MINCED
   TARRAGON

3 OUNCES SHAVED MANCHEGO
   CHEESE

2 EGG YOLKS (OPTIONAL)

In a bowl, add the olive oil, lime zest and juice, anchovy, shallot, tarragon, cheese, and egg yolks. Whisk well until smooth and creamy.

SOFT-POACHED EGGS

Temper the eggs by letting them sit out of the refrigerator for at least 20 minutes before cooking. Boil a small pot of water. Carefully add the eggs. Poach hard in the boiling water for 6 minutes. Remove the eggs from the boiling water and place immediately in an ice bath. Once completely cool, peel off shell, cut the eggs in half, and garnish the salad.

GRILLED FRISÉE
WITH BACON VINAIGRETTE
SERVES 4

Frisée is a slightly bitter, abstract, leafy type of chickory. Although one cannot fry leafy greens with much success, some greens, like frisée, stand up quite well to a little char while enhancing its flavor.

---

4 HEADS FRISÉE

4 SOFT-POACHED EGGS
(PAGE 106)

3 SLICES SMOKED BACON

1 MEDIUM SHALLOT, PEELED
AND MINCED

2 TABLESPOONS DIJON
MUSTARD

1 TABLESPOON HONEY

¼ CUP SHERRY OR CHAMPAGNE
VINEGAR

SALT AND PEPPER, TO TASTE

2 TABLESPOONS EXTRA-VIRGIN
OLIVE OIL

Several hours before you prepare this dish, place the frisée in an ice-water bath and let sit. This will help remove some of the tartness from the greens. Next, prepare the Soft-Poached Eggs and set aside for later use.

Preheat an outdoor grill (page 10).

Remove the frisée from the ice bath, pat the leaves dry, and set aside. Prepare the Bacon Vinaigrette by chopping the bacon into small pieces and placing in a sauté pan over medium heat until the bacon begins to brown. Add the shallot and stir constantly for about 30 seconds. Add the mustard, honey, and vinegar, and whisk until all the flavors have married. Remove the Bacon Vinaigrette from the pan, but reserve in a warm place until ready to use. Adjust seasoning with salt and pepper.

Gently toss the frisée with the olive oil and place on the grill. Allow the leaves to wilt slightly on all sides. Remove from grill and place in a bowl. Toss with the Bacon Vinaigrette. Arrange the salad on a serving platter. Slice the Soft-Poached Eggs in half and garnish the salad. You may also garnish with croutons or grated cheese.

GRILLED TOMATOES
WITH BASIL EMULSION
SERVES 4

There are a few iconic items I believe represent summer: carnivals, boat rides, and fresh ripe tomatoes. Even though you can receive tomatoes delivered right to your doorstep, there's nothing like plucking a fresh beefsteak tomato from your garden that has been vine-ripened by the sun and tended to by your very own hand. Unfortunately, not many people these days have the luxury or time to cultivate their own home garden. That's why across America grocery stores are offering a multitude of tomato varietals. And which tomato is the "best"? Which one should you buy? That's a difficult question to answer. My advice would be to test and judge for yourself. Buy an organic heirloom and a regular Roma. Take them home and taste them side by side. If they're fresh and ripe, both should be delicious enough to stand up on their own. However, I believe charring a tomato heightens the level of complexity in a way that most home cooks aren't accustomed to. If you're like me and enjoy experiencing new flavors, try grilling your tomatoes the next time you're preparing a meal that calls for tomatoes.

---

1 POUND BEEFSTEAK TOMATOES

½ CUP EXTRA-VIRGIN OLIVE OIL

1 CUP BASIL LEAVES, DIVIDED

1 TEASPOON RICE WINE VINEGAR

1 TEASPOON AGAVE SYRUP

½ TEASPOON DRY MUSTARD POWDER (OR WET MUSTARD)

1 LARGE SHALLOT, PEELED AND MINCED

SALT AND CRUSHED BLACK PEPPER

Preheat an outdoor grill (page 10).

Using a sharp knife, quarter the tomatoes and brush them with a little olive oil. Place the flesh-side down on the grill for 1 minute, rotate, and grill for another 1 minute. Turn the tomatoes over and repeat the process. When nicely charred, remove the tomatoes from the grill and allow to cool.

In a kitchen blender, add half of the basil along with the ½ cup olive oil, vinegar, agave, and mustard. Blend the Basil Emulsion until smooth. Chiffonade the remaining basil by rolling the leaves tight and slicing them very thin (about ⅛-inch).

In a mixing bowl, add the grilled tomatoes, shallot, chiffonade basil, and the Basil Emulsion. Toss gently and season to taste with salt and pepper.

SMOKED CORN CHOWDER

MAKES 6 QUARTS

I enjoy preparing daily soups at my restaurant that are approachable and familiar yet unique and not found elsewhere. A few years ago, on a chilly day, I had two new sous-chefs, and we decided to experiment with a chowder. I'm not a native of the South, but I'm pretty sure the folks down there would be proud of the soup we developed.

---

1 POUND SALTED BUTTER

1 LARGE LEEK, CHOPPED
(ONLY THE WHITE PART)

½ POUND BACON

¾ CUP FLOUR

1 CUP DICED CARROT

5 LARGE RUSSET POTATOES,
PEELED AND DICED

5 CUPS SMOKED CORN
(RECIPE FOLLOWS)

2 LARGE POBLANO PEPPERS,
SEEDED AND DICED

6 CUPS WHOLE MILK

6 CUPS CHICKEN OR
VEGETABLE STOCK

2 TABLESPOONS KOSHER
SALT

2 TEASPOONS BLACK PEPPER

In a large pot over medium heat, add and melt the butter. Add the bacon and leek and sweat the leek until translucent. Add the flour and stir constantly until a "roux" has formed and smells nutty, about 5 minutes. Add the carrot, potatoes, corn, peppers, milk, and stock. Bring to a boil, then reduce to a simmer over low. Simmer for about 40 minutes, stirring occasionally so nothing sticks to the bottom of the pot. Season with salt and pepper, and garnish with whatever chopped herbs you have available such as parsley or chives.

SMOKED CORN

MAKES 5 CUPS

It is ideal to use fresh (always), but it's easier for most people to buy 5 cups of frozen corn, which case you can smoke it at 175°F for 15 minutes.

If you are ambitious and want to use fresh, you have to blanch it first. Get a large pot of salted water (½ cup of Kosher salt per gallon of water) to a rolling boil. Drop the corn in for 30 seconds. Remove from water and move to smoker.

SMOKED POTATO SALAD
SERVES 8

Potatoes are a fantastic starch to smoke because their porous flesh has the potential to absorb a lot of flavor. When making this salad, make sure you begin with a good potato. I'm particularly fond of Yukon golds or red potatoes. Both have a high water content, which makes for a moist potato salad. And whether you like your potato salad with or without the potato skins is up to you. I prefer the skin on, plus it makes the salad much more nutritious.

---

4 POUNDS YUKON GOLD POTATOES

2 CUPS MAYONNAISE

½ CUP DILL PICKLES, MINCED

½ CUP MINCED CHIVES

1 TABLESPOON APPLE CIDER VINEGAR

1 TABLESPOON STONE GROUND MUSTARD

5 OUNCES GRATED WHITE CHEDDAR

1 BUNCH WATERCRESS

½ CUP SHAVED RED ONION

COOKED BACON (OPTIONAL)

SALT AND PEPPER, TO TASTE

Scrub the potatoes clean, or peel them, and using a sharp knife, cut each potato into quarters. Add the potatoes to a pot of boiling salted water and boil until the potatoes are soft. Remove the potatoes from the pot and allow them to cool.

Preheat an outdoor smoker to 350°F (page 120).

Place the potatoes in the smoker and smoke the potatoes for 15 minutes.

While the potatoes are smoking, in a bowl add the mayonnaise, pickles, chives, vinegar, and mustard. Mix well to combine. Once the potatoes have smoked and allowed to cool, add them to the bowl and fold in the cheese, watercress, onion, and some cooked bacon, if desired. Season to taste with salt and pepper.

GRILLED & CHARRED FEASTS

BURGERS, CHOPS, MEAT & POULTRY

SMOKED TURKEY BREAST WITH CHARRED APRICOT GLAZE | 115

GRILLED MUSHROOM BURGER | 116

GRILLED BISON BURGER WITH CARAMELIZED ONION JAM
& CHARRED JALAPEÑO AIOLI | 117

GRILLED LAMB WITH CHARRED RAPINI & MINT CHIMICHURRI | 120

SMOKED PORK CHOPS WITH BURNT ORANGE GLAZE & COUS COUS | 122

GRILLED NEW YORK STEAK WITH HASSELBACK POTATOES | 126

SMOKED BONE MARROW SCRAMBLE | 128

ROASTED CHICKEN | 129

PAN ROASTED SQUAB WITH CARAMELIZED APPLES | 130

SMOKED FRIED CHICKEN SANDWICH WITH
CHIPOTLE REMOULADE | 132

SMOKED DUCK BREAST WITH BELUGA LENTILS
& BALSAMIC AGRODOLCE | 134

SMOKED MAC & CHEESE | 136

FISH & SHELLFISH

GRILLED FISH TACOS | 138

SMOKED CLAMS WITH BROWN BUTTER PASTA | 140

CARAMELIZED SCALLOPS WITH TOASTED BARLEY RISOTTO
& NETTLE PESTO | 142

BLACKENED SHRIMP WITH SMOKED GRITS | 144

GRILLED OCTOPUS WITH CORONA BEAN RAGOUT &
SHERRY GASTRIQUE | 145

SMOKED TURKEY BREAST
WITH CHARRED APRICOT GLAZE

SERVES 6

When the pilgrims shared a meal with the Native Americans on that first Thanksgiving, the gathering represented a higher meaning; a way to bring people together. Today, no holiday is more revered for bringing people together on the American calendar than Thanksgiving. However, most people tend to forget that a traditional Thanksgiving dinner can be made any day of the year. It's like the pleasant surprise of having breakfast for dinner.

---

1 OR 2 BONELESS TURKEY BREASTS

ALL PURPOSE BRINE, ENOUGH TO COVER (PAGE 84)

CHARRED APRICOT GLAZE (RECIPE FOLLOWS)

Soak the turkey breasts in the All Purpose Brine for 4 hours in the refrigerator. Remove the breasts from the brine and pat dry. Preheat an outdoor smoker to 225°F (page 12). Place the turkey breasts in the smoker and cook until internal temperature reaches 165°F, about 2 hours. Remove from the smoker and allow to sit for 10 minutes before slicing. Serve with a drizzle of the Charred Apricot Glaze.

CHARRED APRICOT GLAZE

---

6 FRESH APRICOTS

4 TABLESPOONS UNSALTED BUTTER

1 CUP APRICOT JAM

¼ CUP HIGH-QUALITY TEQUILA

2 TEASPOONS WHOLE GRAIN MUSTARD

Preheat an outdoor grill (page 10).

Cut the apricots in half and remove the pits. Place the apricots flesh-side down on the grill and allow to caramelize, about 3 or 4 minutes. Remove from the grill and cut the apricots into a small dice.

In a heavy-bottomed saucepan over medium heat, melt the butter and add the grilled apricots. Allow to cook until the apricots are completely soft, about 10 minutes. Add apricot jam, tequila, and mustard. Stir to combine and let cook for several more minutes. Season to taste, remove from heat, and set aside.

GRILLED MUSHROOM BURGER

SERVES 4

Proteins don't always have to be the star of the show. Well-prepared vegetables can be just as delicious and satisfying as any meat. Selecting your vegetable is important, however. It would be unrealistic to replace a bone-in ribeye with a cucumber and expect the same satisfying result. You can, though, combine vegetables and grains that contain the right amount of umami and density to create a dish that leaves you with the satisfaction that is usually found in meat. The most logical and common replacement for meat is mushrooms. For this dish, the large Portbello is the ideal ingredient.

½ CUP BALSAMIC VINEGAR

1 LARGE SHALLOT, PEELED AND
   MINCED

2 GARLIC CLOVES, PEELED AND
   MINCED

¼ CUP MINCED BASIL

½ CUP OLIVE OIL

2 TEASPOONS KOSHER SALT

1 TEASPOON FRESH CRACKED
   BLACK PEPPER

4 LARGE PORTOBELLO
   MUSHROOMS

4 HAMBURGER BUNS

DESIRED CONDIMENTS

In a bowl, add the vinegar, shallot, garlic, basil, oil, salt, and pepper. Mix well.

Remove the stems from the mushrooms and add the caps to the marinade. Gently toss and let sit for 1 hour.

Preheat an outdoor grill (page 10).

Remove the mushroom caps from the marinade and shake off excess. Transfer the mushrooms to the grill, and grill for 5 to 6 minutes. Turn and grill the other side for another 5 to 6 minutes. Remove from the grill and serve between your favorite burger bun, garnished with your favorite condiments, such as lettuce, tomato, mayonnaise, and onion.

GRILLED BISON BURGER WITH CARAMELIZED ONION JAM & CHARRED JALAPEÑO AIOLI

SERVES 4

The key to success when grilling a burger is the sear. You want the perfect amount of caramelization so when you take that first bite, there's a distinct transition from garnish to meat. Regardless of which direction you choose to go, a properly executed burger will ensure that your guests walk away happy. This recipe is a simple, approachable version of one of my restaurant burgers with a fun twist.

2 POUNDS HIGH-QUALITY GROUND BISON BEEF WITH A HIGH FAT CONTENT

2 TABLESPOONS AVOCADO OIL (OR GRAPESEED OIL)

SALT AND PEPPER, TO TASTE

HAMBURGER BUNS

CARAMELIZED ONION JAM (PAGE 119)

CHARRED JALAPEÑO AIOLI (PAGE 119)

In a mixing bowl, generously season the ground beef with the salt, pepper, and oil. Form patties by scooping about 7 or 8 ounces in your hand and packing it like a baseball. Then set it down and flatten it out like a large hockey puck, leaving them about ¾-inch thick. Let the patties sit at room temperature, as long as you will be grilling them within 1 hour. Otherwise, refrigerate until ready to use.

Prepare an outdoor grill to at least 450°F (page 10).

Season the patties again with salt and pepper and place them over the heat. For medium, grill for 2 minutes, give each patty a quarter turn, then grill for 2 additional minutes. Flip the patties and grill for 3 or 4 minutes. Factor less time for medium-rare and additional time for medium-well or well done. Remove the patties from the grill and let rest. While the patties are resting, drizzle a little oil on the inside of both buns and place on the grill and toast. Assemble the burger with the Caramelized Onion Jam and Charred Jalapeño Aioli, and any additional condiments you prefer.

CARAMELIZED ONION JAM

MAKES ¾ CUP

½ CUP UNSALTED BUTTER

4 LARGE YELLOW ONIONS, PEELED AND SLICED
    THIN (¼-INCH OR LESS)

2 TEASPOONS KOSHER SALT

½ CUP BROWN SUGAR

¼ CUP SHERRY VINEGAR (OR OTHER VINEGAR)

1 TABLESPOON THYME LEAVES

In a large pot or pan, add the butter and warm over medium heat until melted. Add the onions and salt and sweat the onions until they caramelize, about 15 minutes. Add the brown sugar, and cook for another 5 minutes. Add the vinegar and thyme leaves, and keep over the heat until the vinegar has been completely absorbed. Cook for an additional 3 minutes. Set aside and let cool.

CHARRED JALAPEÑO AIOLI

MAKES 2 ½ CUPS

2 JALAPEÑOS, GRILLED AND
    SEEDED

3 LARGE EGG YOLKS

1 TEASPOON DRY MUSTARD

1 TEASPOON KOSHER SALT

1 TABLESPOON WATER

2 CUPS CANOLA OIL

Prepare an outdoor grill or a hot pan over high heat with a little oil. Add the jalapeños and grill or sauté until they are dark and nicely charred. When the peppers are cool enough to work with, remove the seeds and stems. Place the jalapeños in a kitchen blender and blend for 1 minute on high. (Note: At this point you can pass the mixture through a chinois or fine strainer to remove any impurities and return to the blender. Otherwise, leave as is.) Add the egg yolks, mustard, salt, and water and blend for 30 seconds. Next, add the oil, pouring slow to give enough time for the eggs and oil to emulsify. Continue to blend until all the ingredients have been incorporated. (Note: If, at any time, you "break" the emulsification, meaning the eggs and oil have become separated and resemble scrambled eggs, simply remove all the ingredients from the blender, add a teaspoon of water to the blender, and repeat the process by drizzling the previously blended ingredients back into the blender.)

GRILLED LAMB
WITH CHARRED RAPINI & MINT CHIMICHURRI
SERVES 4

When it comes to grilled rack of lamb, there's an almost carnal desire to want to pick up the meat with your hands and rip it off the bone with your teeth, letting the juices flow down your chin, which, of course, you're happy to do. The fact is, eating bone-in lamb is a way for us to connect with our primal roots. A dish like this proves that no matter how much we evolve, no matter how far technology develops, there still is no substitute for feasting on meat from the bone after it's been roasted by the fire. Most lamb racks in grocery stores these days are Frenched, a butchering technique in which the meat, fat, and membranes are removed, giving the rack a cleaner look. When available, choose American lamb, and the more local, the better.

FRENCHED RACK OF AMERICAN LAMB (2–3 BONES PER PERSON; EACH BONE WILL YIELD 3 OR 4 OUNCES OF MEAT)

SALT AND PEPPER

CHARRED RAPINI (RECIPE FOLLOWS)

MINT CHIMICHURRI (RECIPE FOLLOWS)

Prepare an outdoor grill to at least 450°F (page 10).

Place the rack fat-side up on a cutting board. With a very sharp knife, score the fat diagonally ¼ inch apart to create a checker pattern. Season the lamb liberally with salt and pepper.

Place the lamb fat-side down on the grill. (Note: Watch for flare-ups caused by the dripping fat. If a flare occurs, simply move the lamb to another part of the grill.) For medium rare to medium, grill for about 8 minutes, then turn over and grill for another 5 to 6 minutes. Once caramelized and cooked to your desired temperature, remove the lamb from the grill and let rest for 5 minutes before slicing. Serve with the Charred Rapini and Mint Chimichurri.

CHARRED RAPINI

2 BUNCHES RAPINI (OR
    BROCCOLI RABE)

½ CUP OLIVE OIL, DIVIDED

1 LIME, JUICED

SALT AND PEPPER

Prepare an outdoor grill to at least 450°F (page 10).

Bring a large pot of heavily salted water to a rolling boil. While the water is coming to a boil, remove the bottom 1 inch of the rapini. Next, prepare an ice bath.

Once the water is boiling, add the rapini and boil for 30 seconds. Remove the rapini and place into the ice bath for at least 10 minutes. Remove the chilled rapini from the water and pat dry.

In a bowl, add the rapini along with ¼ cup of the oil and season with salt and pepper. Toss well. Transfer the rapini to the grill. (Note: Watch for flare-ups caused by the dripping oil. If a flare occurs, simply move the rapini to another part of the grill.) Grill the rapini for 3 minutes, then turn over and grill for another 3 minutes. Transfer the grilled rapini back to the bowl, and toss them with the remaining oil along with the lime juice. Season again with salt and pepper.

MINT CHIMICHURRI
MAKES 1½ CUPS

1 CUP MINT LEAVES

¼ CUP CILANTRO LEAVES

½ CUP OLIVE OIL

½ CUP EXTRA-VIRGIN OLIVE OIL

1 GARLIC CLOVE, PEELED

1 MEDIUM SHALLOT, PEELED
    AND CHOPPED

1 TEASPOON LIME JUICE

1 LIME, ZESTED

1 TEASPOON KOSHER SALT

In a kitchen blender or food processor, add the mint, cilantro, oils, garlic, shallot, lime juice, lime zest, and salt. Blend until smooth.

SMOKED PORK CHOPS
WITH BURNT ORANGE GLAZE & COUS COUS
SERVES 4

Statistically, pork is the number-one consumed protein in the world, accounting for 36 percent of all meat consumption. In the United States, it's ranked third. With many different cuts of hog, combined with the techniques we're illustrating in this book, the cooking possibilities are endless. It's also worth noting that as a pig matures, so does its muscular system, which in turn, strengthens the connective tissue. This tissue, which creates a stronger flavor, is difficult to break down with a quick, high-heat process. For cuts like the butt and shoulder, the best cooking method is to braise at a lower temperature to make the cuts more palatable. Cuts like the loin and tenderloin, however, never develop muscle due to their placement in the skeletal structure of the animal, which makes them naturally very tender. These are the cuts that benefit from a quick, high-heat method such as grilling or roasting, as you'll find in this recipe.

---

4 BONELESS (OR BONE-IN) PORK CHOPS

1 TABLESPOON ONION POWDER

1 TABLESPOON GARLIC POWDER

1 TABLESPOON SMOKED PAPRIKA

1 TABLESPOON KOSHER SALT

1 TABLESPOON FRESH CRACKED BLACK PEPPER

½ CUP OLIVE OIL

BURNT ORANGE GLAZE (RECIPE FOLLOWS)

COUS COUS (RECIPE FOLLOWS)

Preheat an outdoor smoker to 225°F (page 12).

In a small bowl, add the onion powder, garlic powder, smoked paprika, salt, and pepper. Mix well to combine. Rub the pork chops generously with the mixture.

Place the seasoned pork chops on a smoking tray, and smoke for 30 minutes. Remove from the smoker and place in the refrigerator. (Note: These steps can be done up to a day ahead of time.)

Once ready to prepare and serve the dish, preheat an outdoor grill (page 10).

Place the seasoned chops on the grill and cook for about 6 minutes on each side. Use an internal thermometer to ensure the meat reaches 155°F. (Note: Cooking times will vary, depending on the size of chops.) Remove from the grill and drizzle the Burnt Orange Glaze over the top of the chops. Serve with the Cous Cous.

BURNT ORANGE GLAZE

1 CUP AGAVE SYRUP

4 ORANGES

CANOLA OIL, AS NEEDED

2 CLOVES

1 STICK CINNAMON (OR
½ TEASPOON GROUND
CINNAMON)

1 TEASPOON KOSHER SALT

1 TABLESPOON WHOLE
PEPPERCORNS (OR ½
TEASPOON FRESH GROUND
BLACK PEPPER)

Peel the oranges, and reserve the peels.

Add enough oil to a sauté pan to just coat the bottom, and bring to medium-high heat. Add the peeled oranges (Note: You will need a kitchen tool like tongs to continually turn the oranges.) Toast the oranges while continually turning them until the oranges are darkened on all sides. Remove from the heat and squeeze the juice from the oranges, reserving the juice.

In a saucepan over medium-high heat, add the orange juice, syrup, cloves, cinnamon, salt, and peppercorns. Simmer for 10 minutes. Remove from heat and strain using a chinois or kitchen strainer. Allow the syrup to cool.

COUS COUS

2 TABLESPOONS UNSALTED
BUTTER

1 LARGE SHALLOT, PEELED AND
MINCED

2 GARLIC CLOVES, PEELED AND
MINCED

1 CUP COUS COUS

2 CUPS CHICKEN OR VEGETABLE
STOCK

1 TABLESPOON KOSHER SALT

1 CUP MINCED FRESH HERBS
(CHIVES, PARSLEY,
TARRAGON)

2 TABLESPOONS LEMON JUICE

½ CUP OLIVE OIL

In a saucepot over medium-low heat, melt the butter and add the shallot and garlic. Sweat the shallot and garlic for 5 minutes, or until they become translucent.

Warm a pot over medium heat. Add the cous cous and toast for 5 minutes. Add the stock and salt, bring to a boil, then remove from the heat. Cover and let sit for 5 minutes. Remove the cous cous from the pot, transfer to a serving bowl, and let cool. Once cool, add the herbs, lemon juice, and olive oil. Adjust seasoning if necessary.

GRILLED New York STEAK
WITH HASSELBACK POTATOES
SERVES 2

Of the countless dishes I've had the pleasure of preparing for my father over the years, his favorite is still grilled New York steak. There's something about a good juicy steak that reminds him of his childhood. For this recipe, I like serving the New York with Swedish-style baked potatoes. They take a little patience to prepare, but they're worth it.

---

2 (1-INCH-THICK) NEW YORK
    STEAKS (PREFERABLY GRASS
    FED)
2 TABLESPOONS CANOLA OIL
SALT AND PEPPER
HASSELBACK POTATOES (RECIPE
    FOLLOWS)

Let the steaks sit at room temperature for 1 hour before grilling. Preheat an outdoor grill to high heat (page 10). Brush both sides of the steaks with oil and generously season with salt and pepper. On the hottest part of the grill, add the steaks. For medium-rare, grill for 2 or 3 minutes. Rotate 45 degrees and grill for another 2 to 3 minutes. Turn the steaks over and repeat the process. After both sides are grilled and cooked to your desired doneness, remove the steaks and let rest for 5 minutes under loosely fitted aluminum foil. Serve with the Hasselback Potatoes.

HASSELBACK POTATOES

---

4 RUSSET POTATOES (MEDIUM
    TO LARGE SIZE)
⅓ CUP CANOLA OIL
½ POUND MELTED UNSALTED
    BUTTER
KOSHER SALT AND PEPPER
¼ CUP MINCED TARRAGON
¼ CUP MINCED CHIVES

Preheat the oven to 450°F. Scrub the potatoes clean. Using a very sharp knife (important), slowly cut vertically all the way down as close to the bottom of the potato without cutting through. Repeat this process, leaving a ¼ inch between each cut.

Transfer the potatoes to a parchment-lined roasting tray. Combine the oil and melted butter and pour over the potatoes, making sure the mixture gets in between all the slices. Season with salt and pepper. Roast in the oven for about 50 minutes, or until the potatoes open like a fan and turn golden brown. Remove from the oven and garnish with the tarragon and chives. (Note: You can add other garnishes, such as sour cream, cheese, bacon, etc.)

SMOKED BONE MARROW SCRAMBLE

SERVES 2

Edible bone marrow is the interior tissue of a cow bone, usually the femur or humerus, that becomes soft and delicious when exposed to heat. Its uses are vast. Those who are familiar with bone marrow don't often associate marrow with breakfast. In this recipe, you'll find bone marrow works as a fantastic base for scrambled eggs. Just remember bone marrow has the melting characteristics of butter, meaning that when exposed to heat, the marrow will melt.

---

1 POBLANO PEPPER

1 RED BELL PEPPER

4 LARGE EGGS

2 OUNCES SMOKED BONE MARROW (PAGE 81)

1 SMALL SHALLOT, PEELED AND MINCED

2 OUNCES COTIJA CHEESE

1 TABLESPOON MINCED TARRAGON

1 TEASPOON KOSHER SALT

½ TEASPOON FINELY CRUSHED BLACK PEPPER

Preheat the oven to 500°F.

Place the Poblano and red bell pepper on a roasting tray and roast in the oven for 12 minutes. Turn the peppers over and roast for another 15 minutes. Remove the peppers from the oven and transfer to a bowl and cover. Let sit for 15 minutes. Under running water, remove the seeds and stems from the peppers and scrape off the skin. Cut the peppers into a small dice.

In a bowl, add the eggs and use a fork to lightly aerate. Using a nonstick pan, melt the bone marrow over medium heat. Add the shallots and peppers and cook for 3 minutes, stirring frequently to prevent burning. Add the eggs and slowly stir constantly using a spatula. When the eggs are almost cooked, add the cheese and tarragon and continue cooking to desired doneness. Remove from heat and season with salt and pepper to taste.

ROASTED CHICKEN

SERVES 6

To me, a perfectly roasted chicken is a dish of beauty. A moist chicken breast with crispy skin can turn the dinner table silent as everyone stops to savor their bites. Try to always select a quality bird. Do your research and find a high-quality sustainable product that will suit your personal needs and align with your own standards. (An excellent book for learning more about chicken and sustainable poultry is the James Beard Award–winning title *Culinary Birds*, which happens to be cowritten by my coauthor of this book.) You should also never rinse your chicken. I see home cooks do this all the time. All you're doing is spreading germs in a large radius outside of your sink. When it comes to serving your perfectly roasted chicken, you can either carve and serve the chicken immediately, or you can store the chicken for up to three days and serve hot or cold. If you'd like, you can make a delicious pan sauce to accompany the bird by straining and collecting the juice and bits from the roasting pan, placing it in a pan over medium heat and adding some butter. For example, if you collect about ¾ cup of liquid, you will need ¼ cup of butter. Simply slice the butter into small pieces and add to the pan with the liquid, making sure to swirl the pan to incorporate.

---

1 ORGANIC CHICKEN
  (3–4 POUNDS)

⅔ CUP MELTED UNSALTED
  BUTTER

1½ TABLESPOONS KOSHER SALT

1 TEASPOON FRESH GROUND
  BLACK PEPPER

1 LARGE LEMON

2 TABLESPOONS FRESH THYME
  LEAVES

2 SPRIGS ROSEMARY

6 SMASHED GARLIC CLOVES

Preheat the oven to 425°F.

Pat the chicken dry (do not rinse) and transfer to a cooking rack or a parchment-lined roasting tray. Completely coat the outside of the chicken with the melted butter. Let sit for several minutes to allow the butter to cool and solidify to the skin. Squeeze the lemon juice over the top of the chicken and place the lemon into the chicken cavity. Sprinkle the salt, pepper, and thyme over the chicken. Add the rosemary and garlic cloves to the inside cavity. Transfer to the center rack of the oven. Roast for 25 minutes, then turn the roasting tray and roast for another 15 minutes. Check the internal temperature of the chicken by using a kitchen thermometer to ensure the chicken has reached 165°F. You can also check by poking a thick part of the chicken like the breast. If the juices run clear, the chicken is done. If not cooked, place the chicken back in the oven, and check every 5 minutes until done. Remove the chicken from the oven, loosely place a piece of aluminum foil over the top, and let sit for 15 minutes before serving.

PAN ROASTED SQUAB
WITH CARAMELIZED APPLES
SERVES 4

A squab is a young domesticated pigeon—and a true delicacy. Resembling the flavor and texture of dark chicken meat, squab isn't commonly found in homes or restaurants across the country. The window of cooked perfection also isn't as large as we would like it to be. This is due to two primary factors: (1) Because squab are smaller and more dainty than the average chicken, they tend to cook faster; and (2) Squab is (preferably) cooked from medium rare to medium, so getting the cooking time down can be a bit tricky. Nevertheless, this dish is worth trying and perfecting for family and friends.

4 SQUAB

KOSHER SALT

CRUSHED BLACK PEPPER

CANOLA OIL, AS NEEDED

½ CUP UNSALTED BUTTER

2 APPLES (GRANNY SMITH),
  PEELED AND CUT INTO
  ½-INCH CUBES

1 TEASPOON THYME LEAVES

¼ CUP WHITE BALSAMIC
  VINEGAR

Preheat the oven to 450°F.

Carefully remove the back bone from the squab and press the bird down lightly to flatten. Season generously with salt and pepper. Coat the bottom of a cast-iron or sauté pan with a little canola oil and bring to high heat. Once the pan is hot, place the squab skin-side down for 2 minutes. Carefully turn the birds over and immediately transfer to the oven for 8 minutes. Remove the birds from the oven and place over medium-high heat. Add the butter and lower the heat the medium-low. Add the apples and thyme, and carefully tilt the pan. Using a large spoon, ladle the brown butter over the birds for 2 minutes. Set the pan back down flat, add the vinegar, and cook for 30 seconds. Remove the pan from the heat and allow to rest for 5 minutes. Transfer the birds to a serving platter and garnish with the caramelized apples and pan sauce.

SMOKED FRIED CHICKEN SANDWICH
WITH CHIPOTLE REMOULADE
SERVES 2

Fried chicken sandwiches are one of those comfort dishes that can go miraculously wrong in an instant. From under-seasoned to over-cooked, a poorly prepared fried chicken sandwich is nothing short of a tragedy. The key to successfully frying chicken is soaking the bird in buttermilk. Buttermilk contains lactic acid, which helps marinate, brine, and add flavor to chicken. Creating a quality dredge is equally important. In this recipe, I also smoke the chicken, which creates yet another amazing level of flavor without drying out the meat.

---

2 ORGANIC CHICKEN BREASTS

2 CUPS BUTTERMILK, DIVIDED

1 TABLESPOON SALT

**1 TABLESPOON CRACKED BLACK
PEPPER**

**CHICKEN DREDGE (RECIPE
FOLLOWS)**

**CHIPOTLE REMOULADE (RECIPE
FOLLOWS)**

SANDWICH BREAD, AS NEEDED

**SANDWICH CONDIMENTS, AS
NEEDED**

Preheat an outdoor smoker to 165°F (page 12).

In a saucepot, add 1 cup of the buttermilk along with the salt and pepper. Bring to a boil over high heat, then immediately remove from the heat. Transfer the hot buttermilk to a separate container and add the remaining cup of buttermilk. Let the mixture cool.

Using a sharp knife, gently filet each chicken breast in half with the knife parallel to the cutting board or surface area. Arrange the chicken filets on a smoking tray and place in the smoker for 20 minutes. Remove the chicken and let cool. Add the chicken to the buttermilk mixture and allow to sit for 3 hours to up to 24 hours.

Preheat the oven to 350°F.

Remove the chicken from the buttermilk and shake off excess. Dredge in the Chicken Dredge mixture and transfer to a baking sheet. Place in the oven and bake until crispy and the chicken is cooked throughout, about 6 to 8 minutes.

When ready to assemble, take your favorite sandwich bread and spread both sides with Chipotle Remoulade (Note: Hoagies, French rolls, and sliced bread works well). Add the fried chicken and garnish with your favorite sandwich toppings, such as shredded lettuce, fresh tomato slices, and grilled onions.

CHICKEN DREDGE

2 CUPS ALL-PURPOSE FLOUR

1 TABLESPOON CAYENNE PEPPER

1 TABLESPOON GROUND DRY
   MUSTARD

1 TABLESPOON GARLIC POWDER

1 TEASPOON KOSHER SALT

1 TEASPOON CRACKED BLACK
   PEPPER

In a bowl, add the flour, cayenne, mustard, garlic, salt, and pepper. Mix well to combine.

CHIPOTLE REMOULADE

1 CUP MAYONNAISE

1 LIME, ZESTED AND JUICED

1 LARGE SHALLOT, PEELED AND
   MINCED

1 TABLESPOON MINCED CHIVES

1 TABLESPOON MINCED
   CILANTRO

2 TABLESPOONS CHIPOTLE
   PASTE

1 TEASPOON KOSHER SALT

1 TEASPOON CRACKED BLACK
   PEPPER

In a bowl, add the mayonnaise along with the lime zest and juice, shallot, chives, cilantro, chipotle paste, salt, and pepper. Mix well to combine.

SMOKED DUCK BREAST
WITH BELUGA LENTILS & BALSAMIC AGRODOLCE

SERVES 6

Smoked duck is one of my favorite dishes. Ever since I was a child, I would ask for smoked duck on my birthday. The juicy flavor combination of sweet and smoky with its slight gaminess is something I have always enjoyed. Try this recipe and you may enjoy it, too.

6 DUCK BREASTS

ALL PURPOSE BRINE, ENOUGH
    TO COVER (PAGE 84)

CANOLA OIL, AS NEEDED

BELUGA LENTILS (RECIPE
    FOLLOWS)

BALSAMIC AGRODOLCE (RECIPE
    FOLLOWS)

Soak the duck breasts in the All Purpose Brine for a minimum of 6 hours in the refrigerator, but preferably overnight. (Note: If you leave the duck in the brine too long, the breasts will become too salty and take on a ham-like texture.)

Preheat an outdoor smoker to 175°F (page 12).

Remove the breasts from the brine and rinse well with cold water. Place the breasts skin-side up on a cutting board and, using a very sharp knife, score the skin a ½ inch apart all the way across, going both ways, to make a checkered pattern. Cut all the way through the skin but do your best not to cut through the meat.

Place the duck breasts in the smoker for 40 minutes. At this point, you can either cook the duck right away or refrigerate them for later use. The duck will stay fresh for up to 4 days.

When you are ready to cook and serve, preheat the oven to 425°F.

Pat the duck breasts dry to remove as much moisture from the skin as you can. Using a cast-iron pan (stainless will work in a pinch), over high heat, coat the bottom with just enough canola oil to cover. When the oil is hot, add one duck breast at a time. Leave on high heat to let the pan come back up to temperature after all the breasts have been added (about 30 seconds), then transfer the pan to the oven for 8 to 10 minutes. Remove the pan from the oven and set aside. When ready to serve, either slice the breasts into ½-inch thick slices or serve whole. Serve with the Beluga Lentils and drizzle the Balsamic Agrodolce over the top of the duck.

BELUGA LENTILS

1½ CUPS RINSED BELUGA
LENTILS
3¼ CUPS CHICKEN STOCK (OR
VEGETABLE STOCK)
1 TABLESPOON KOSHER SALT
1 CUP SMALL DICE MIREPOIX
(ONIONS, CARROTS, CELERY)
CANOLA OIL, AS NEEDED

In a large sauce pot, add the lentils, stock, and salt. Bring to a boil and reduce to a simmer. While the lentils are simmering, add a small amount of canola oil to a sauté pan and bring to high heat. Once the pan is hot enough to make water sizzle, add the mirepoix and sauté, stirring frequently to prevent browning, for about 3 minutes. Remove from heat and set aside while the lentils finish cooking, about 25 minutes total. Once the lentils are tender but not mushy, add the sautéed mirepoix and season to taste.

BALSAMIC AGRODOLCE

½ CUP BALSAMIC VINEGAR
¼ CUP WHITE SUGAR

In a saucepan, add the vinegar and sugar. Stir and bring to a boil over high heat. Boil hard for 3 minutes. Remove from heat and set aside to cool. Once cool, drizzle the syrup over the duck.

SMOKED MAC & CHEESE

SERVES 6

There's nothing more American than a bowl of Mac & Cheese. What's beautiful about this meal is that no two are alike. With so many different varieties of pastas and cheeses to choose from, there is virtually an endless amount of possibilities. I discovered Smoked Mac & Cheese some years ago when I attended a friend's wedding. The food was catered by a BBQ truck. There were ribs, both beef and pork, baked beans, rolls, coleslaw, and then the piece de resistance, this delectably smoked macaroni and cheese. I have eaten quite a few meals in my life, and this dish is definitely in my top ten for most memorable foods of all time.

---

10 OUNCES UNCOOKED PASTA
(ELBOW OR ORECCHIETTE)

½ CUP UNSALTED BUTTER

3 TABLESPOONS ALL-PURPOSE
FLOUR

3 CUPS WHOLE MILK

1 CUP CREAM CHEESE

2 CUPS GRATED CHEDDAR
CHEESE

2 TABLESPOONS MINCED
TARRAGON

½ CUP BREAD CRUMBS

CHERRY TOMATOES, HALVED
(GARNISH, OPTIONAL)

Bring a pot of salted water (make it taste like the ocean) to a boil. Add the pasta and cook until al dente. Drain the pasta from the water and allow to cool.

In a saucepan, melt the butter over medium heat and add the flour. Using a high-heat resistant spatula, stir the roux consistently for 3 to 5 minutes, or until the butter and flour smells nutty. Slowly pour in the milk and whisk well until the mixture comes to a simmer. Add the cheeses and continue whisking until the cheeses are melted, then add the tarragon. Transfer the pasta to a casserole dish and pour the cheese mixture over the top. Mix gently to combine. Spread the bread crumbs evenly over the top.

Preheat an outdoor smoker to 200°F (page 12).

Place the casserole dish in the smoker for 45 minutes. Remove from smoker and serve immediately. Garnish with halved cherry tomatoes, if desired.

GRILLED FISH TACOS
SERVES 4

Spending time with my family in Washington's San Juan islands and catching our dinner by way of the sea are memories I will always cherish. Depending on the season, the main ingredient was salmon, cod, or halibut. Often, my mother would grill tomatoes and chilies over a beach fire to make fresh salsa. She would also set up a comal and make fresh tortillas. I understand this is a luxury not available to everyone, but if you buy fresh, quality seafood and share it with family and friends, you too will create wonderful memories.

---

1 POUND FRESH WILD
    SUSTAINABLE FISH (HALIBUT,
    MAHI-MAHI, SEA BASS)

¼ CUP CANOLA OIL

½ CUP LATIN RUB (PAGE 34)

2 LARGE TOMATOES

½ CUP DICED RED ONION

1 BUNCH MINCED CILANTRO

1 JALAPEÑO, SEEDED AND
    MINCED (OPTIONAL)

2 TABLESPOONS LIME JUICE

1 TEASPOON KOSHER SALT

8 CORN OR FLOUR TORTILLAS

1 CUP SHAVED CABBAGE (RED
    OR GREEN)

Prepare an outdoor grill (page 10).

Coat the fish with the oil and the Latin spice rub, and set aside at room temperature. Seed and dice the tomatoes. In a bowl, add the tomatoes, onion, cilantro, jalapeño, lime juice, and salt. Place the fish on the grill and allow to char on one side. Turn over and continue to grill until the flesh is opaque and cooked through. Remove the fish from the grill and set aside. Place the tortillas on the grill and allow to char slightly on one side. Remove the tortillas and set aside. To assemble, tear away the fish using a fork and place on top of the grilled tortilla. Add some of the shredded cabbage on top of the fish, and garnish with the tomato salsa.

SMOKED CLAMS
WITH BROWN BUTTER PASTA
SERVES 6

Pasta with clams is very delicious on its own, but pasta is unique in the sense that it's a vessel for almost anything you have available to you depending on the time of year. You can add roasted root vegetables in the winter, fresh tomatoes from the garden in the summer, and everything in between. Eating well also doesn't have to be expensive. Both pasta and clams are relatively inexpensive so learning how to make this magnificent dish will bring countless cherished memories to the dinner table. Enjoy a delicious, decadent, creamy, and buttery pasta dish with this recipe.

---

4 POUNDS CLAMS

**1 POUND SHELL PASTA
(OR ANY TYPE)**

¾ POUND UNSALTED BUTTER

½ CUP CHOPPED TOMATOES

¼ CUP CHOPPED TARRAGON

½ CUP GRATED PARMESAN

Preheat an outdoor smoker to 300°F (page 12).

Purge the clams by running them under cold water for 10 minutes to remove any sand. Transfer the clams from the water directly into the smoker for 30 minutes. Bring a large pot of salted water to a boil. Place the pasta in the boiling water and keep the rolling boil until the pasta is cooked through and al dente, about 5 minutes. Strain the pasta and set aside. In a large sauce pot, melt the butter over medium-high heat until the butter browns. Add the pasta to the browned butter. Add the smoked clams (Note: Discard any unopen clams), along with the tomatoes, tarragon, and cheese. Season to taste. Served with grilled French baguette.

CARAMELIZED SCALLOPS
WITH TOASTED BARLEY RISOTTO & NETTLE PESTO
SERVES 4

Scallops are often referred to as "Sea Candy," and for good reason. These delicious morsels are packed with sweet and salty goodness. Paired with a pesto made from stinging nettles, which are sought after for their superior nutritional value, this dish is as close as you will come to the Pacific Northwest on a plate. When cooking scallops, I suggest pulling them off the heat right before you think they are ready, as an undercooked scallop is still delicious, while an overcooked scallop is not.

CARAMELIZED SCALLOPS
1 POUND (BETWEEN 10 AND 20)
FRESH SEA SCALLOPS
CANOLA OIL, AS NEEDED
SALT AND PEPPER, TASTE
¼ POUND UNSALTED BUTTER

NETTLE PESTO
1 POUND STINGING NETTLES
2 GARLIC CLOVES
1 SMALL SHALLOT
½ CUP OLIVE OIL
½ CUP PINE NUTS
ZEST FROM 1 LIME
1 TEASPOON LIME JUICE
SALT AND PEPPER, TO TASTE

Generously coat the bottom of a cast-iron pan with canola oil over medium heat. Season the scallops with salt and pepper. When hot, carefully, and one at a time, place the scallops in the pan. Allow them to caramelize on one side for about 45 seconds. Add the butter to the pan and flip the scallops over one at a time. Allow the butter to brown. Tilt the pan (Note: Use a kitchen towel if the handle is hot) so all the browned butter pools into one corner of the pan. Using a large spoon, baste the brown butter over each scallop. Continue basting for about 1 minute. Immediately remove the scallops from the pan and place them on paper towels to absorb some of the extra butter. Season again with salt and pepper.

To make the Nettle Pesto: Bring a large pot of water to a rolling boil and prepare an ice bath. Carefully add the nettles and boil for 1 minute. Remove the nettles and immediately place in the ice bath. Once cool, remove as much water as you can from the nettles by squeezing them between paper towels. Add the nettles to food processor along with the garlic, shallot, olive oil, pine nuts, lime zest, and juice. Pulse until a paste-like consistency is achieved. Season with salt and pepper to taste.

Toasted Barley Risotto

5 CUPS CHICKEN OR VEGETABLE
STOCK

1 CUP SALTED BUTTER

2 CLOVES GARLIC, PEELED AND
MINCED

1 LARGE SHALLOT, PEELED AND
MINCED

1 TABLESPOON MINCED THYME
LEAVES

2 CUPS BARLEY

½ CUP CHOPPED CHIVES

1 TABLESPOON EXTRA-VIRGIN
OLIVE OIL

SALT AND PEPPER, TO TASTE

To make the Toasted Barley Risotto: In a pot over high heat, add the stock and bring to a boil. Remove from heat and set aside. In a saucepot over medium heat, add the butter. When melted, add the garlic and shallot. Sweat the garlic and shallot for about 5 minutes until they become translucent. Add the thyme leaves and sweat for 1 minute. Add the barley. Toast the barley for about 3 minutes, just to get a little color. Reduce heat to medium-low. Add 2 cups of the stock and stir until all the liquid is absorbed. Keep adding 1 cup at a time until all the liquid is absorbed. Stir frequently so the bottom doesn't scorch, and reduce heat if necessary. Once all the liquid is absorbed, add the chives and olive oil. Season to taste with salt and pepper.

To serve, place 1 large scoop of the Toasted Barley Risotto on a dinner plate, arrange 3 or 4 scallops on the risotto, and place 1 teaspoon of the Nettle Pesto over each scallop. Serve while warm.

BLACKENED SHRIMP WITH SMOKED GRITS
SERVES 8 [4 SHRIMP PER PERSON]

This down-home Southern country favorite is a crowd pleaser and for good reason. The combination of well-seasoned shrimp paired with the creaminess from the Smoked Grits creates an extraordinary palate experience. As always, make sure to buy the best prawns available so the result will be as good as possible. Personally, I like sustainable cold-water prawns like the spot prawns found in the Pacific Northwest as opposed to the farm-raised warm-water varieties, which can be mushy and not environmentally friendly.

---

1 CUP COURSE GROUND GRITS

4 CUPS WHOLE MILK

1 TABLESPOON KOSHER SALT

¼ POUND UNSALTED BUTTER, CUBED SMALL

6 OUNCES GRATED WHITE CHEDDAR

2 TABLESPOONS MINCED TARRAGON

SALT AND PEPPER, TO TASTE

32 LARGE PRAWNS, SHELLS REMOVED AND DEVEINED

BLACKENING SPICE, AS NEEDED (PAGE 30)

Preheat an outdoor smoker to 250°F (page 12).

Arrange the coarse ground grits flat on a sheet tray and place in the smoker for 20 minutes. Remove from smoker.

In a large saucepan over medium heat, add the milk and salt. Slowly add the smoked grits a little at a time, stirring constantly until the mixture is smooth. Turn the heat to low and stir constantly until the grits are creamy, about 15 minutes. Once creamy, add the butter, cheese, and tarragon. Season to taste with salt and pepper.

Add the shrimp to a bowl and dredge heavily with the Blackening Spice. Add enough oil to just cover the bottom of a cast-iron skillet over medium-high heat. When hot, add the shrimp and cook for about 2 minutes on each side. Remove the shrimp from the skillet and place on top of the smoked grits.

GRILLED OCTOPUS WITH CORONA BEAN RAGOUT & SHERRY GASTRIQUE

SERVES 8

This has been my best-selling dish at the restaurant for the last several years. The sear from caramelizing the octopus, combined with the creaminess from the Corona Bean Ragout and the sweet and sour flavor of the Sherry Gastrique creates an almost mind-blowing culinary experience.

---

4 POUNDS WHOLE UNCOOKED OCTOPUS (PORTUGUESE)

2 CUPS WHITE WINE

½ CUP KOSHER SALT

1 LEMON, CUT IN HALF

1 LIME, CUT IN HALF

1 ORANGE, CUT IN HALF

4 TEASPOONS ALEPPO POWDER (1 TEASPOON PER POUND OF OCTOPUS)

COLD WATER, AS NEEDED

1 TABLESPOON CANOLA OIL

BEAN RAGOUT (RECIPE FOLLOWS)

SHERRY GASTRIQUE (RECIPE FOLLOWS)

In a stock pot, add the octopus, wine, salt, lemon, lime, orange, and Aleppo powder. Add some cold water until the octopus is submerged. Bring to a boil over high heat. When boiling, reduce to a simmer and cook for 2½ hours. Keep adding water if necessary. Once the octopus is tender, remove from the braising liquid and pat the octopus dry. Once cool, remove the tentacles from the octopus by placing the entire octopus flat on a cutting board and using a sharp knife to work around the head. Discard the head.

Bring a sauté pan up to medium heat with the canola oil. Add the octopus tentacles to the pan and sauté until crispy, making sure to turn the tentacles over and crisp all sides before serving with the Bean Ragout and a drizzle of the Sherry Gastrique.

CORONA BEAN RAGOUT

MAKES 5 CUPS

4 CUPS SOAKED CORONA
BEANS

1 CUP ROUGHLY
CHOPPED MIREPOIX
(ONIONS, CARROTS,
CELERY)

5 BAY LEAVES

¼ CUP PEPPERCORNS

1 BUNCH THYME

1 GALLON COLD WATER

½ CUP SALT

½ POUND SALTED
BUTTER

SOFRITO (RECIPE
FOLLOWS)

Soak the beans overnight in water. Once soaked, drain and add to a large stock pot. Using a piece of cheesecloth, bundle the mirepoix, bay leaves, peppercorns, and thyme into a sachet. Add to the pot along with the water and salt. Bring to a boil, then reduce to a simmer. Cook until the beans are tender, about 1½ hours. Drain the beans, reserving a little of the liquid. Transfer the beans and the liquid back to the pot. Just before serving, heat the beans and fold in the butter and Sofrito.

SOFRITO

MAKES 1½ CUPS

2 LARGE PEELED AND SMALL
DICED YELLOW ONIONS

2 PEELED AND MINCED GARLIC
CLOVES

4 OUNCES SALTED BUTTER

2 OUNCES TEQUILA (REPOSADO)

1 BUNCH CHOPPED CILANTRO

ZEST FROM 1 LIME

1 TABLESPOON SALT

In a sauté pan, add the butter and melt over medium heat. Add the onions and garlic, and cook until the onions are translucent. Watching carefully, bring the heat to high to caramelize the onions. Once they begin to caramelize, remove the pan from the heat, add the tequila, and bring the pan back to the heat. Next, proceed with caution. If you have a gas range, the alcohol will ignite on its own; if electric, use a match or lighter to ignite the alcohol. Once the pan is aflame, allow the alcohol to burn off, then remove the pan from the heat and let cool. Fold in the cilantro, lime zest, and salt.

SHERRY GASTRIQUE

1 CUP GRANULATED SUGAR

1 CUP SHERRY VINEGAR

In saucepot, add the sugar and just a little water to hydrate it. Cook over medium heat, stirring constantly, until the water has evaporated and the sugar starts to caramelize. Just before the sugar burns, add the vinegar. The mixture will instantly harden. Keep over the heat until the mixture boils. Immediately remove from the heat. Transfer to another vessel and chill before using.

BLISTERED & GRILLED SIDES

SWEETENED BROWN BUTTER CARROTS | 149

BLISTERED CORN WITH MAYONNAISE, QUESO & CHILE | 150

BLISTERED PEPPERS WITH CHARRED SCALLION REMOULADE | 152

BURNT AVOCADO TOAST | 154

CHARRED SUMMER SQUASH | 155

CRISPY BRUSSELS SPROUTS WITH ORANGE HABANERO GASTRIQUE
& SMOKED PINE NUTS | 156

GRILLED SWEET POTATO WITH ROSEMARY BROWN BUTTER | 158

GRILLED HARICOTS VERTS WITH GARLIC CONFIT | 159

GRILLED PEACHES WITH PROSCIUTTO, BURRATA
& JEREZ GASTRIQUE | 160

GRILLED RED CABBAGE SLAW WITH BURNT
HONEY VINAIGRETTE | 162

GRILLED STRAWBERRY SALAD WITH MINT DRESSING | 164

GRILLED WATERMELON SALAD | 166

SWEETENED BROWN BUTTER CARROTS
SERVES 4

When roasted, these Sweetened Brown Butter Carrots showcase an umami flavor that is so deep and rich it's almost as if they have a meat-like quality to them. Topping the carrots with the nutty brown butter, or *beurre noisette*, makes them all the more decadent. It's important to remember when making this side that you shouldn't add too much char or you'll ruin the flavor of the carrots. What I enjoy about this side is that these carrots are easy to make and you can pair them with almost anything. Whether it's an elegant Chateaubriand or a simple meat loaf, roasted carrots with brown butter are definitely a welcome accoutrement. And while traditional orange carrots will work just fine, get creative and use this recipe with a rainbow of different colored carrots.

---

2 POUNDS CARROTS

¼ CUP UNSALTED BUTTER

¼ CUP HONEY

1 TABLESPOON SHERRY VINEGAR

¼ CUP CRUSHED WALNUTS

1 TEASPOON KOSHER SALT

1 TEASPOON FRESH GROUND BLACK PEPPER

2 TABLESPOONS MINCED CHIVES

Preheat the oven to 400°F.

Peel the carrots and cut them on a bias, about 1-inch thick. If you are using baby carrots, still peel, but leave them whole. Place the carrots in a large bowl and set aside.

In a small saucepan, warm the butter and honey over medium heat until the butter starts to brown. Add the vinegar and the walnuts and stir together. Pour the mix over the carrots and gently toss together. Arrange on a parchment-lined roasting tray and place in oven for 15 to 20 minutes. Remove from the oven and season with the salt and pepper. Transfer the carrots to a serving tray and garnish with the chives.

BLISTERED CORN
WITH MAYONNAISE, QUESO & CHILE

MAKES 6 SERVINGS

Some of my fondest memories as a child was when my mother would give me a few pesos to run down to any street corner in Mexico to get an *elote*. This street-food favorite is sold in two forms: grilled or boiled. If you ask me, there's no question as to which one is better. The little specks of charred kernels add a level of flavor you cannot get from boiling. This Latin American favorite is found everywhere. Whether you're at street fairs, graduations, Quinceañeras, or Sunday suppers, elote, in some form, is sure to be present. It's also a side dish that has managed to transcend above all. From the poorest of the poor, to the president himself, not a person in Mexico doesn't enjoy the indulgence of fire-roasted corn, slathered in chile and mayonnaise and eaten right off the cob. You might get a little messy,
but I promise it's well worth it.

---

6 WHOLE CORN (INCLUDING
   HUSK)

½ CUP MAYONNAISE

½ CUP MEXICAN CREMA (OR
   SOUR CREAM)

1 TEASPOON GARLIC POWDER

1 TEASPOON ONION POWDER

½ CUP CRUMBLED COTIJA OR
   QUESO FRESCO

2 TABLESPOONS CHILE POWDER

1 BUNCH MINCED CILANTRO

KOSHER SALT

This can be done over a gas or charcoal grill, but to get that truly authentic flavor, I recommend charcoal.

Light a grill and get it to at least 450°F if using gas, or smoldering coals if using charcoal. While the grill is warming up, pull back the husks on all the corn, leaving them still intact and on the cob. Using a dry towel, pull the threads from the kernels themselves and set aside. In a mixing bowl, combine the mayonnaise, crema, and two powders until it is a homogenous mixture. Once the grill is hot, put the corn over the heat, leaving the husk handles over the edge so they don't burn. Rotate every few minutes, until all sides of the corn have a little char on them. How long will depend on the heat of your grill, but it should take no more than 6 or 7 minutes. Once charred, remove from heat, and over a clean surface slather the corn with the mayonnaise mix. Then roll the corn in the crumbled cheese, sprinkle with the chile powder and cilantro, season generously with salt, and enjoy.

BLISTERED PEPPERS
WITH CHARRED SCALLION REMOULADE
SERVES 8

This recipe calls for Padrón peppers (a small Spanish pepper that are mild except for the occasional scorcher). Padróns are easily interchangeable with Shishitos (a sweet, Asian pepper), which are more seasonal and more readily available than the Padrón. The key to effective blistering and caramelization is getting the pan hot, adding the peppers, and then not touching the pan until necessary.
If you shake the pan, all you're doing is tossing the peppers around while cooling the entire pan, thereby negating why you got the pan hot in the first place.

---

2 QUARTS PADRÓN (OR
    SHISHITO) PEPPERS
½ CUP CANOLA, AVOCADO, OR
    GRAPESEED OIL
SALT AND PEPPER, TO TASTE
CHARRED SCALLION
    REMOULADE (RECIPE
    FOLLOWS)

In a mixing bowl, toss the peppers with the oil, salt, and pepper. Heat a large cast-iron pan over medium-high heat. Water should sizzle when you flick some onto the pan. Add the peppers to the pan and do not move the peppers for 20 seconds. After 20 seconds, carefully shake the pan around to agitate the peppers and get a char on all sides of the peppers. This process should take no more than 5 minutes. Make sure not to overcook the peppers or they will get too wilted. Remove the peppers from the heat and transfer back to the bowl. Season again with salt and pepper. Serve warm with a side of Charred Scallion Remoulade.

CHARRED SCALLION REMOULADE
MAKES 1½ CUPS

---

1 CUP MAYONNAISE
2 TABLESPOONS WHOLE GRAIN
    MUSTARD
2 TEASPOONS CHAMPAGNE
    VINEGAR (OR WHITE WINE
    OR RICE WINE VINEGAR)
1 TABLESPOON SRIRACHA

1 LARGE PEELED AND MINCED
    SHALLOT
1 TABLESPOON CHOPPED
    TARRAGON
5 GRILLED AND CHOPPED
    SCALLIONS
SALT AND PEPPER, TO TASTE

In a bowl, combine the mayonnaise, mustard, vinegar, Sriracha, shallot, tarragon, scallions, salt, and pepper. Mix well and chill for at least 1 hour before serving.

BURNT AVOCADO TOAST
SERVES 4

Avocado toast has swept the United States and abroad. The exact origin is unknown, but countries where avocadoes grow native have been mashing and serving them on vessels like bread and toast for centuries. Today, people, particularly millennials, are swapping out the drive-through fried egg sandwich and coffee for avocado toast and a soy latte. Recently, I asked my father what he thought of avocado toast. His response was priceless. "What the heck is avocado toast?" Avocado toast, in my humble opinion, is unique in the sense that it is accepted by all, regardless of economic stature, social class, or food preference. It's loved by nobility, vegans, hipsters, the wealthy, the poor, and everyone in between. The beautiful part about this side is that there is no set recipe, no specific procedure or protocol you need to follow. Really all you need are some ripe avocados and a high-quality bread. I serve this recipe for Avocado Toast at my restaurant. It's simple, yet elegantly delicious.

---

4 LARGE RIPE HASS AVOCADOS

1 LARGE MINCED SHALLOT

1 TABLESPOON MINCED CHIVES

⅓ CUP MAYONNAISE

ZEST AND JUICE FROM 1 LIME

2 TEASPOONS SALT

4 SLICES WHEAT BREAD (OR
    YOUR FAVORITE VARIETY)

Preheat an outdoor grill (page 10) or cast-iron pan.

Halve the avocados and remove the pits. Once smoking hot, place the avocados flesh-side down and allow to fully char. The meat will turn black and bubble, and this is what you want. Once charred, remove from heat and set aside to cool.

In a mixing bowl, add the shallot, chives, mayonnaise, lime zest and juice, and salt. Mix well.

Using a small spoon, scoop out the meat from the avocados, small pieces at a time, about the size of a marble, and add to the mixture. Using the same spoon, mix and slightly mash the mixture until everything is well incorporated. Adjust seasoning to taste.

Place the bread in a preheated oven or toaster just enough to warm and slightly brown the bread. Spread the avocado mixture over the toast and serve.

CHARRED SUMMER SQUASH

SERVES 6

Squash, a versatile vegetable that holds up to many cooking methods—grilled, fried, sautéed, braised, or even shaved thin and eaten raw—is fantastic year-round. In this recipe, I'm grilling the squash over high heat to caramelize the natural sugars while pairing it with some chopped epazote, which goes perfectly with grilled squash. For those not familiar, epazote is an herb used exclusively in southern Mexican and Guatemalan cuisine. Epazote has a flavor profile similar to oregano with an almost menthol-like quality. Epazote can be difficult to find but well worth the search. If you can't find epazote at a specialty spice- or Mexican store, you can order online.

---

3 POUNDS SUMMER SQUASH

1 CUP OLIVE OIL, DIVIDED

1 TABLESPOON FRESH LIME JUICE

1 TABLESPOON AGAVE SYRUP

1 LARGE MINCED SHALLOT

2 TEASPOONS KOSHER SALT

1 TEASPOON FRESH CRACKED BLACK PEPPER

½ CUP FRESH CHOPPED EPAZOTE

¼ CUP MINCED CHIVES

½ CUP MEXICAN CHEESE (QUESO FRESCO OR COTIJA)

Preheat an outdoor grill (page 10).

Trim the squash by cutting a ½ inch off both ends, then cut in half the long way. Toss the halves with ½ cup olive oil. Place the squash flat-side down on the grill, and cook for 3 minutes. Rotate 45 degrees and grill for another 3 minutes. Turn the squash over and grill for 5 minutes. Depending on the temperature of your grill, the squash should develop a good char. Once cooked to desired doneness, set aside and let the squash come to room temperature.

In a bowl, add the remaining ½ cup olive oil along with the lime juice, agave syrup, shallot, salt, and pepper. Mix well until emulsified.

Cut squash into smaller pieces, about the width of your thumb. Toss with the dressing to coat. Add the epazote, chives, and cheese. Toss again and adjust the seasoning to your likeness.

CRISPY BRUSSELS SPROUTS WITH ORANGE HABANERO GASTRIQUE & SMOKED PINE NUTS

SERVES 4

Brussels sprouts are arguably the most disliked vegetable among children, but one of the more versatile and well-liked veggies by adults. I must agree with the kids: boiled in water, these brassicas are almost unpalatable. When introduced to a high-heat cooking method, such as roasting, frying, grilling, or sautéing, something magical happens to the Brussels sprout. The caramelized leaves from the small edible buds exude a pleasant and unique umami flavor. Personally, I enjoy cutting Brussels sprouts in half and deep-frying them until the outer leaves are crispy, which is the recipe I provided. If you don't have access to a deep-fryer, you can also roast them. Blanching and grilling also work well if you have a vegetable rack that will fit over your grill and keep them from falling through the grates. Whichever way you decide to prepare Brussels sprouts, please don't simply boil them in unseasoned water and cover them with bacon bits. Anyone who grew up in the United States knows exactly what I'm talking about.

CANOLA OIL, AS NEEDED, FOR DEEP-FRYING

2 POUNDS BRUSSELS SPROUTS

ORANGE HABANERO GASTRIQUE (RECIPE FOLLOWS)

SMOKED PINE NUTS (RECIPE FOLLOWS)

Preheat a deep-fryer with oil to 350°F.

Using a sharp knife, trim the bottom of the Brussels sprouts along with the outside leaves and discard. Cut the sprouts in half, lengthwise, through the core. Place the sprouts in a fryer-safe basket into the deep fryer. Completely submerge the Brussels sprouts for 45 seconds and remove from the oil. Transfer to a bowl and toss with the Orange Habanero Gastrique and Smoked Pine Nuts. Serve warm.

ORANGE HABANERO GASTRIQUE

MAKES 1 CUP

½ CUP SUGAR

⅓ CUP ORANGE JUICE

⅓ CUP SHERRY VINEGAR

2 HABANERO PEPPERS, SEEDED
AND MINCED

In a heavy-bottomed sauce pot, add the sugar and warm over medium heat while stirring constantly with a high-temperature spoon or spatula until the sugar dissolves. Continue stirring until the sugar is golden brown, about 5 minutes. Quickly and carefully, add the orange juice and sherry vinegar. Note: The sugar will harden. Continue stirring occasionally over medium heat for another 10 minutes to allow the sugar and liquids to become a homogenous mixture. Once a complete liquid, carefully transfer to another container and set aside to let cool. Once completely cool, stir in the minced habaneros.

SMOKED PINE NUTS

MAKES 1 CUP

1 CUP PINE NUTS

2 TABLESPOONS OLIVE OIL

½ TEASPOON SALT

½ TEASPOON PEPPER

Preheat an outdoor smoker to low heat (page 12).

Arrange the pine nuts evenly on a smoker-safe tray. Smoke for 10 minutes. Once smoked, allow the nuts to cool.

Preheat the oven to 350°F.

Place the pine nuts in a bowl and toss with the olive oil, salt, and pepper. Transfer back to the sheet pan and roast in the oven for 6 minutes, rotating the pan halfway through.

GRILLED SWEET POTATO
WITH ROSEMARY BROWN BUTTER

SERVES 4

Sweet potatoes are usually thought of as a winter dish (especially during Thanksgiving and Christmas dinners), but they are a year-round item. This tuber, which is only a distant relative to its non-sweet counterpart, the potato, can withstand high heat. Grilling sweet potatoes is an excellent option, as caramelizing the natural sugar found in this root vegetable will provide a pleasant texture and flavor contrast.

---

4 LARGE SWEET POTATOES

½ CUP CANOLA OIL

1 TABLESPOON KOSHER SALT

4 OUNCES UNSALTED BUTTER

1 SPRIG FRESH ROSEMARY

1 TABLESPOON AGAVE SYRUP

¼ CUP MINCED MIX OF MINT AND CHIVES

Preheat grill or oven to 400°F.

Scrub the potatoes well and cut into wedges, so the width is about ½ to ¾ inch. Add the potato wedges to a bowl and toss with the canola oil and salt.

Arrange the wedges on either the grill racks or roasting trays. For the grill, allow to caramelize on both sides, but not burning, until you can push a toothpick all the way through without any resistance, about ½ hour. If roasting in the oven, roast for 15 minutes, remove the tray, turn the potato wedges over, and roast for an additional 15 minutes.

While the potatoes are cooking, place the butter in a saucepan over medium-high heat. As the butter begins to melt, add the rosemary and agave syrup. Watch the butter carefully; as soon as it begins to smell nutty and turn brown, carefully remove the rosemary from the butter and transfer the butter to another pan to stop the cooking process. Once the potatoes are done, add them to the butter mixture, along with the mint and chives. Season to taste with additional salt.

GRILLED HARICOTS VERTS WITH GARLIC CONFIT

SERVES 4

Classical French dishes, like this one, are classical for a reason. They're like classic cars; they never go out of style. If you can't find fresh haricots verts—they're simply a slender French green bean—you can easily swap them for the common green bean.

1 POUND HARICOTS VERTS, STEMS REMOVED

1 TEASPOON KOSHER SALT

1 TEASPOON FRESH GROUND BLACK PEPPER

2 TABLESPOONS EXTRA-VIRGIN OLIVE OIL

¼ CUP UNSALTED BUTTER

GARLIC CONFIT (RECIPE FOLLOWS)

Preheat outdoor grill (page 10).

Heavily salt a large pot of cold water and bring to a rolling boil over high heat. Add the beans and cook for 3 minutes. Remove the beans from the water and transfer to an ice bath for 3 to 5 minutes to stop the cooking process. Remove the beans from the ice bath and place on a towel to dry. Transfer the beans to a bowl and toss with the salt, pepper, and olive oil. Place on the grill and char for about 3 minutes. Remove the beans and transfer back to the bowl. Melt the butter and add to the bowl with the Garlic Confit. Toss well. Season to taste.

GARLIC CONFIT

¾ CUP PEELED GARLIC CLOVES

2 CUPS CANOLA OIL

Preheat the oven or outdoor grill to 250°F (page 10).

Put the garlic cloves and oil in an oven-safe container and roast for 2 hours. Remove the cloves from the heat and oil and allow to cool. Once cooled, place the garlic on a cutting board and smash each clove with the side of the knife. Toss the smashed garlic with the Grilled Haricots Verts.

GRILLED PEACHES WITH PROSCIUTTO, BURRATA & JEREZ GASTRIQUE

SERVES 4

When the season allows, grilled stone fruit is one of those luscious culinary bites people find so delectable, and one of the easiest side dishes to execute. Grilled fruit also pairs well with cheese plates, charcuteries, pork chops, salads, virtually anything. As for the peach, once grilled, the fruit is very well-rounded on the palate. The natural sweetness and tanginess from the peach and the umami from the char create an almost whimsical experience. I find peaches work best among stone fruits for grilling due to their natural firmness. Coating them with oil and quickly roasting over high heat is the ideal way to accomplish the perfect char. In this recipe, I'm using prosciutto, but you can also use Jamón Serrano, the Spanish equivalent. Same with the vinegar. Any vinegar will work so long as it's not distilled. If you'd like to keep with a Spanish theme, try Jerez, a unique Spanish sherry vinegar that hails from the same region.

---

2 RIPE PEACHES

½ CUP OLIVE OIL

SALT AND PEPPER, TO TASTE

⅓ CUP GRANULATED SUGAR

½ CUP JEREZ SHERRY VINEGAR (OR OTHER NON-DISTILLED VINEGAR)

4 OUNCES FRESH BURRATA

6 SLICES PROSCIUTTO

½ CUP CHIFFONADE FRESH BASIL

½ CUP TOASTED PINE NUTS

Preheat an outdoor grill (page 10).

Slice the peaches into quarters and remove the pit. Cut the quarters in half. Add the peaches to a bowl, add the olive oil, and season with salt and pepper. Toss to combine. Shake off excess and place the peaches on the grill. Allow one side to caramelize (about 3 to 4 minutes), then turn and caramelize the other sides following the same procedure. Remove the peaches from the grill and allow to cool.

In a small sauce pot, add the sugar and a just small amount of water (just enough to hydrate the sugar). Over medium-high heat, allow the water to evaporate, as the sugar will begin to caramelize. Once the sugar is amber-brown, add the vinegar. The sugar will harden, which is okay. Allow the ingredients to reheat and return to a homogenous mixture. Remove the caramelized sugar from the heat and allow to cool completely. This will turn the sugar into a syrup-like consistency.

To serve, place the burrata in the center of the plate. Arrange the grilled peaches around the burrata, along with the prosciutto. Drizzle the Jerez Gastrique over the top, and garnish with the basil and pine nuts.

GRILLED RED CABBAGE SLAW
WITH BURNT HONEY VINAIGRETTE
SERVES 6

What I like about coleslaw is that it's so versatile. Cabbage is wonderful on almost any type of sandwich—a fantastic accoutrement to almost any protein, as well as satisfying on its own. Sure, there is nothing wrong with shredding some raw cabbage and mixing it with a mayonnaise-based dressing, but I'm sure you've realized by now that is not the direction we've been taking. Grill it, roast it, or even sauté it, and you might like what you discover when heating cabbage. For this recipe, I grill the cabbage, but feel free to roast it in the oven at high-heat, or place the cabbage in a covered pan with some liquid, some aromatics, and braise it.

1 LARGE HEAD RED CABBAGE

½ CUP OLIVE OIL

½ CUP BROWN SUGAR

1 TEASPOON SALT

1 LARGE PEELED AND MINCED
    SHALLOT

BURNT HONEY VINAIGRETTE, AS
    NEEDED (RECIPE FOLLOWS)

Preheat an outdoor grill (page 10).

Remove the outer, dirty leaves from the cabbage and discard. Slice the cabbage head into 6 equal pieces, cutting through the core.

In a bowl, whisk the olive oil, brown sugar, salt, and shallot together until combined. Add the cabbage and toss to evenly coat.

Place the cabbage onto the grill for 2 minutes, then turn 45 degrees and grill for an additional 2 minutes. Turn the cabbage pieces over and repeat the process. When finished, remove the cabbage from the grill, place in a suitable container, and cover with plastic wrap or aluminum foil. Let sit for 15 minutes. Then remove the cabbage from the container and allow to come to room temperature. Dress with the Burnt Honey Vinaigrette and serve.

BURNT HONEY VINAIGRETTE

MAKES 2 CUPS

½ CUP HONEY

½ CUP CHAMPAGNE VINEGAR

½ CUP CANOLA OIL

½ CUP OLIVE OIL

1 TABLESPOON DIJON MUSTARD

1 TABLESPOON MINCED
   SHALLOT

1 TABLESPOON MINCED CHIVE

1 TEASPOON SALT

In a small pot or sauté pan over medium heat, add the honey and carefully toast for about 5 minutes, agitating constantly. Remove the honey from the heat and add to a mixing bowl. Add the vinegar, oils, mustard, shallot, chive, and salt. Whisk together until emulsified.

GRILLED STRAWBERRY SALAD
WITH MINT DRESSING
SERVES 6

Grilling fruit is a fantastic way to enhance the flavor of an already exceptional product. Caramelizing the natural sugars will invite a different experience to the palate in both flavor and texture. Strawberries especially benefit from this caramelization process, as the fructose develops over the heat, and combined with the natural tanginess of the strawberry, provides an unexpected bite.

½ CUP AGAVE SYRUP

½ CUP BALSAMIC VINEGAR

¼ CUP OLIVE OIL

1 PINT CLEANED AND TRIMMED
    FRESH STRAWBERRIES

½ PINT FRESH BLACKBERRIES

½ PINT FRESH RASPBERRIES

2 BUNCHES WATERCRESS

⅓ CUP SHAVED RED ONION OR
    SHALLOT

4 OUNCES TOASTED AND
    CRUSHED HAZELNUTS,
    DIVIDED

1 TEASPOON KOSHER SALT

1 TEASPOON CRACKED BLACK
    PEPPER

3 OUNCES CRUMBLED FETA

MINT DRESSING (RECIPE
    FOLLOWS)

In a bowl, add the agave syrup, balsamic vinegar, and olive oil. Toss well to combine. Next, cut the strawberries in half and add to the bowl. Coat the berries well and transfer the bowl to the refrigerator for 1 hour.

Remove the strawberries from the bowl and shake off excess marinade. Reserve the marinade for later use.

Preheat an outdoor grill to medium heat (page 10).

Gently arrange the berries in the center of the grill and allow to caramelize. Using tongs, rotate the berries so they caramelize equally on all sides. Be careful not to go too far or they become mushy. Remove from grill and allow to cool.

Once the strawberries are cool, gently toss them in a bowl with the blackberries, raspberries, watercress, onion, half of the hazelnuts, Mint Dressing, and the salt and pepper. Place in a serving bowl and garnish with the remaining hazelnuts, feta, and the balsamic marinade.

MINT DRESSING
MAKES 1 1/2 CUPS

½ CUP BUTTERMILK

⅓ CUP MAYONNAISE

⅓ CUP OLIVE OIL

1 CUP FRESH MINT LEAVES

1 LARGE PEELED SHALLOT

1 TEASPOON LEMON JUICE

1 TEASPOON KOSHER SALT

1 TEASPOON CRACKED BLACK
   PEPPER

To make the Mint Dressing, add to a kitchen blender the buttermilk, mayonnaise, olive oil, mint, shallot, lemon juice, salt and pepper. Pulse on high until the dressing is completely emulsified.

GRILLED WATERMELON SALAD
SERVES 8

One question I often hear is "What else should I serve at my barbecue?" One side I always recommend is Grilled Watermelon Salad, because this salad is delicious, refreshing, and simple to make. Next time you're shopping for that backyard picnic, skip over those bags of premade coleslaw and buy yourself a nice plump, dark green, hollow-sounding watermelon. I promise, grilling watermelon will be one of the easiest tasks you'll complete at your next barbecue. Because of its high water content, watermelon is difficult to burn, and thanks to its high sugar content, the melon caramelizes very well when it meets a hot grill.

---

1 (6–8 POUNDS) MEDIUM
   WATERMELON
½ CUP EXTRA-VIRGIN OLIVE OIL
½ CUP BALSAMIC VINEGAR
¼ CUP CHOPPED MINT
¼ CUP CHOPPED BASIL
¾ CUP ARUGULA
½ CUP FETA CHEESE
KOSHER SALT
CRACKED BLACK PEPPER
½ CUP CRUSHED NUTS
   (OPTIONAL)

Preheat an outdoor grill (page 10).

Cut the watermelon into large round discs, each about 1-inch thick, leaving the rind intact.

Place the watermelon slices on the grill, and let cook for 2 minutes. Turn the slices over and repeat the process. When the slices are nice and caramelized, remove them from the grill and let cool. Using a sharp knife, carefully remove the rind from the watermelon and cut the flesh into cubes. Discard the rind.

In a large bowl, combine the olive oil and vinegar. Add the watermelon along with the mint and basil, and gently toss. Add the arugula and feta and gently toss again. Season with salt and pepper, and add some crushed nuts, if desired.

CHARRED & TOASTED DESSERTS

BANANAS FOSTER

SERVES 4

This is one of those "proceed with caution" recipes, and here's why: There was a point in my career when I was that chef with the tall pointy hat who worked a bananas Foster station during a hotel banquet. I had set up my little station and got ready for service. The banquet captain was nice enough to lend me an assistant so I wouldn't have to scoop the ice cream while I was lighting the dessert on fire. About an hour in, it was business as usual. I kept flambéing, and guests kept coming. There came a moment when I added the rum, tilted the skillet, but nothing happened. So I added some more rum, and still nothing. In hindsight, I should have abandoned the assembly at this point, but I didn't. I added a little more rum, tilted the skillet, and POOF! A small meteor-sized ball of flame erupted, scorching my chef coat, and worse, the hair on my face! I didn't panic, however. I calmly turned to the assistant and asked, "Am I on fire?" She replied "No," so I continued about my business. I learned two lessons that day: 1) if you cannot get the rum to light the first time, stop and start the dessert over, and 2) eyelashes don't grow back the same once they've been burnt off.

---

2 OUNCES UNSALTED BUTTER

1 CUP BROWN SUGAR

1 TEASPOON CINNAMON

⅓ CUP BANANA LIQUEUR

2 BANANAS SLICED ½-INCH THICK ON A BIAS

⅓ CUP DARK RUM

BROWN BUTTER ICE CREAM (PAGE 170) OR SMOKED ICE CREAM (PAGE 181), AS NEEDED

In a sauté pan, melt the butter over medium heat. Add the brown sugar and cinnamon and allow the sugar to dissolve. Add the banana liqueur and bananas and cook for 2 minutes, stirring constantly. Remove the pan from the heat and add the dark rum. Return pan to the heat and bring the heat up to medium-high. If you are using a gas range, carefully tilt the pan slightly until the alcohol catches fire. If you are using an electric range, you will have to manually (and carefully) light the flambé with a long reach lighter. Once the pan is ablaze, use a slow swirling motion with your wrists to agitate the mixture. Once the flame is out, carefully scoop out the contents and transfer to an ice cream bowl that has been filled with a couple scoops of ice cream. Serve immediately.

BROWN BUTTER ICE CREAM
MAKES 1½ QUARTS

Toasting butter is a great trick chefs frequently use that you might enjoy as well. Browning butter is the process of taking whole butter, removing the water over the heat, and then toasting the milk solids and butterfat until the butter has a dark color and nutty aroma. At home, I keep a small jar of brown butter next to the stove to use as a quick flavoring agent to almost anything. One of my favorites is adding a small amount to some toast sprinkled with a little sugar and cinnamon. This recipe for Brown Butter Ice Cream is quite simple to execute, and once you finish your first batch, you'll likely turn around and make another batch. The beauty in this ice cream is its versatility. My family enjoys the ice cream with a little cinnamon, fresh fruit, or bananas.

---

8 TABLESPOONS SALTED BUTTER

1 CUP BROWN SUGAR

1 TEASPOON SALT

6 LARGE EGG YOLKS

SEEDS FROM 2 VANILLA BEANS

1 WHOLE MILK

2 CUPS HEAVY CREAM

Add the butter to a sauce pot over medium heat. Stir constantly until you see little brown flakes and the butter takes on a nutty aroma. Remove from heat and stir in the brown sugar and salt. Let sit until the mixture cools, about 30 minutes.

Add the brown butter mixture to a kitchen mixer and process on medium speed. While still on medium, add the egg yolks, one at a time, and mix until there aren't any lumps. Return the mixture to the sauce pot, add the vanilla, milk, and cream, and bring to a boil over medium heat, stirring constantly. The ice cream base is done when the whisk leaves a trail in the cream. Strain and let cool for several hours. Use an ice cream maker and spin until consistency of soft serve. Freeze until ready to use.

CHARRED PAVLOVA
SERVES 8

This Pavlova dessert is named after the ballerina Anna Pavlova, and it's incredibly delicious. Pavlova, incidentally, is a light meringue-like dessert, traditionally topped with whipped cream and fresh berries. Egg whites are whipped hard with acid and caster sugar, then baked at a low temperature until the outside is crispy and the inside texture remains soft, like marshmallow. This is a fantastic dessert to assemble and serve to those guests who enjoy decadence and sophistication without all the unnecessary calories. My advice with this dish is to master how to make the Pavlova, then experiment with different toppings. Grill some papaya, smoke strawberries, toast honey, and see what different flavor combinations you can come up with.

6 EGG WHITES

½ TEASPOON CREAM OF TARTAR

½ TEASPOON VANILLA EXTRACT

1 CUP CASTER SUGAR

1 TEASPOON CORNSTARCH

FRESH FRUIT, DRIZZLE OF HONEY OR AGAVE SYRUP (OPTIONAL)

Preheat the oven to 350°F.

In a kitchen mixer with the whisk attachment set on high, add the egg whites, cream of tartar, and vanilla extract and whip until foamy. Lower the speed to medium and slowly incorporate the sugar and cornstarch. Return the speed to high and whip for 5 minutes, or until the whites are smooth and glossy.

Place the mixture into a piping bag and cut off ¾ inches from the bottom of the bag. Pipe about ½ cup of mixture at 1 inch high onto a parchment-lined sheet tray, leaving at least 2 inches between each amount. Using a spoon, insert into the middle of the piped mixture, and pull it out while grabbing some of the mixture to create peaks. Do as many as you would like to eat. This next step is optional: If you have a kitchen torch available, quickly torch the outside of the "meringues" by holding the torch about 6 inches away and quickly going back and forth to quickly char just the tips of the peaks.

Place sheet tray in oven and roast for 10 minutes. Reduce the temperature to 300°F and roast for an additional 45 minutes. Turn off the oven but leave the meringues inside. Allow to cool inside the oven for about 30 minutes. Remove from oven and serve with the fresh fruit and a drizzle of honey or agave syrup, if desired. If you are not going to consume them the day you make them, store them in an airtight container with silica packets. The meringues will stay fresh for up to 2 days.

GRILLED PEACH TART

SERVES 8

One food I identify the beginning of summer with is stone fruit, and in this case, peaches. They are a versatile fruit and there's so much you can do with them. Everything from jams, to salads, to grilling so you can place them on top of proteins—peaches can easily find a home in the culinary world. While stone fruit is fantastic on its own, giving the fruit a little char provides you with caramelized morsels of charred sweetness. Because of modern-day farming practices and importation, you're often able to get peaches and other stone fruits year-round, but to really enjoy the best possible fruit, try and stick to purchasing peaches in the summer months when the sun has a chance to work its magic. This recipe is for a Grilled Peach Tart, but I promise, once you have grilled a fresh ripe peach at home, you're going to want to add it on everything—salads, pizzas, entrees, and, of course, desserts.

3 FRESH RIPE PEACHES

2 TABLESPOONS CANOLA OIL

1 TEASPOON CINNAMON

⅓ CUP GRANULATED SUGAR

2 TABLESPOONS ALL-PURPOSE FLOUR

¼ TEASPOON FRESH GROUND NUTMEG

1 TEASPOON KOSHER SALT

½ TEASPOON CAYENNE (OPTIONAL)

1 LARGE EGG

1 REFRIGERATED PIE CRUST, THAWED

WHIPPED CREAM (GARNISH, OPTIONAL)

Preheat an outdoor grill (see page 10).

Slice the peaches in half, remove the seeds, and cut the flesh of each peach half into quarters, leaving you with 12 pieces. Toss the peaches with the canola oil and place on the hottest part of the grill. Allow the peaches to caramelize on both, about 4 minutes each. Remove from grill and allow to cool. Once cool, slice the peaches in half again, now leaving you with 24 pieces. Transfer the peaches to a bowl and add the cinnamon, sugar, flour, nutmeg, salt, and cayenne. Toss well.

Preheat the oven to 350°F.

Lay the pie crust out flat on a parchment-lined roasting pan and place the peach mixture in the center, leaving a 1½ inch border all the way around. Crack the egg into a bowl and whisk hard using a fork. Brush the border of the pie crust with the egg wash. Fold the pie crust in an overlapping pattern all the way around, covering the edge of the peaches. Cook in the oven for 30 minutes. Remove and allow to sit for 10 minutes before slicing to allow the mix to harden. Serve on its own or garnish with a dollop of whipped cream.

GRILLED STRAWBERRY PIE

SERVES 8

I will admit I was somewhat skeptical the first time I heard about grilling a strawberry pie. I was catering one of the annual farm dinners I often do in Washington state. One of my very dear friends, who runs a certified organic farm, also grows a lot of beautiful strawberries. I remember her throwing a dozen raw strawberry pies on the grill right after I had pulled off some nice racks of lamb. She smiled and said, "Just you wait and see!" She was right. Pure deliciousness.

---

3 CUPS FRESH RIPE
   STRAWBERRIES
⅓ CUP SMOKED SUGAR (RECIPE
   FOLLOWS)
1 TABLESPOON CORNSTARCH
¼ CUP FRESH STRAWBERRY JAM
1 REFRIGERATED PIE CRUST,
   THAWED
WHIPPED CREAM (OPTIONAL)

Preheat an outdoor grill to 350°F (page 10). Wash, halve, and then remove the stems from the strawberries. Add to a bowl and combine with the Smoked Sugar and cornstarch.

Spread the strawberry jam over the bottom of the pie crust, leaving an inch at the edge clean. Place the strawberries in the center of the crust and fold the crust one pinch at a time to the center. Continue all the way around, leaving about a 4-inch hole in the middle, exposing the strawberries. Place the entire pie on the center of the grill and roast for about 20 minutes. Remove from the grill and allow to cool slightly before cutting. Garnish with whipped cream, if desired.

SMOKED SUGAR

There's no magic or glory behind smoking sugar. It's about as simple as it gets. Use in any recipe that calls for regular sugar and see how it changes the depth of flavor. Incorporating smoked sugar is also a great way to add a little umami flavor to dishes that might otherwise be lacking in that department. Either way, having a little smoked sugar on hand is never a bad thing.

---

2 CUPS GRANULATED SUGAR

Preheat an outdoor smoker to 350°F (page 12). Place the sugar in an even layer across a roasting tray. Place the tray in the smoker and set a timer for 30 minutes. The sugar should have a nice brown color from the smoke. Remove the sugar from the smoker and allow to cool completely before placing in an airtight container. Reserve until ready to use. The sugar will stay fresh for up to 30 days.

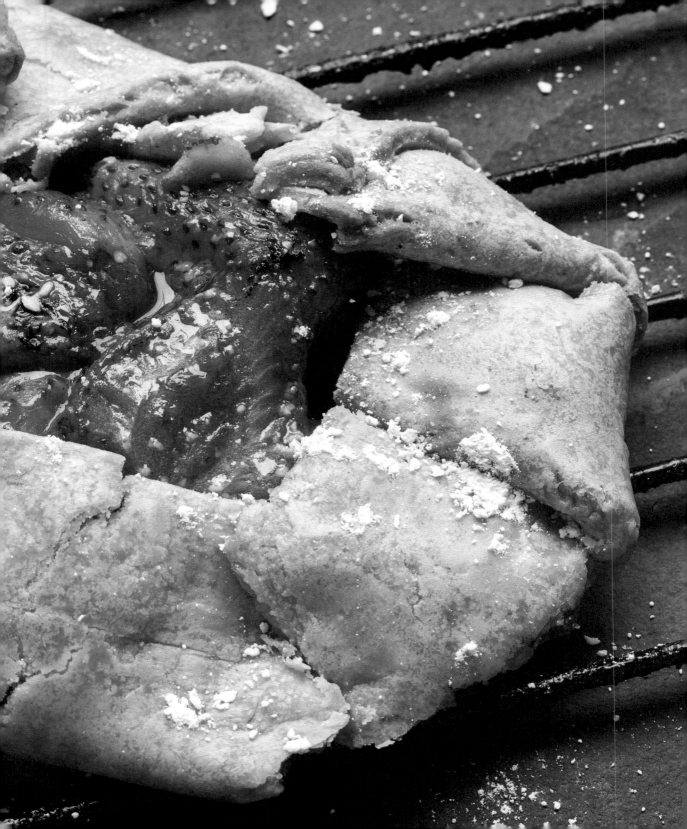

S'MORES WITH SMOKED MERINGUE
SERVES 8

As we mature into adulthood, we sadly tend to leave behind many of the culinary treats we used to enjoy as children. The question I ask is, why not continue to enjoy them? Sometimes all it takes is a whimsical reinvention of a classic to convince our older, more mature selves that it's socially acceptable to partake in a children's diet. A classic example of this is fettucine Alfredo, which is simply mac and cheese for grown-ups. Another is s'mores. When I was a young boy in the Boy Scouts, I would take monthly camping trips with my fellow troops. During the evenings, we would make s'mores over the campfire using cheap chocolate, a value pack of off-brand marshmallows, graham crackers, and a stick. When I first began creating dessert menus for restaurants some years ago, I came to the realization that my guests loved my whimsical reinterpretations of comfort foods, so I created the adult version and named it S'mores with Smoked Meringue.

CHOCOLATE MOUSSE

5 EGG YOLKS

5 TABLESPOONS WHITE SUGAR, DIVIDED

2 CUPS HEAVY CREAM, DIVIDED

SEEDS FROM 1 VANILLA BEAN (OR 1 TEASPOON EXTRACT)

8 OUNCES BITTERSWEET CHOCOLATE

SMOKED MERINGUE

4 EGG WHITES

¼ TEASPOON CREAM OF TARTAR

¾ CUP SUGAR

1 VANILLA BEAN (OR 1 TEASPOON EXTRACT)

Begin by making the Chocolate Mousse. In a small saucepan, whisk together the egg yolks, 2 tablespoons sugar, and 1 cup of the cream over medium heat. Stir constantly until the whisk leaves a trail in the cream, about 3 or 4 minutes. Remove from heat and whisk in the chocolate and vanilla. Place back on low heat for seconds at a time, if necessary, to melt the chocolate.

Using a kitchen mixer, whip the remaining cup of cream and the remaining sugar on medium-high speed until stiff peaks are formed. Fold in the whipped cream with the chocolate mixture, and allow to cool in the refrigerator.

To make the Smoked Meringue: Preheat oven to 225°F. Separate the egg yolks from the egg whites. Place the egg whites in an outdoor smoker for 15 minutes. Place the egg whites and cream of tartar in a kitchen mixer with the whisk attachment and place on high. Mix until foamy. While the mixer is still on, add the sugar, a little at a time, until all the sugar is incorporated. Add the vanilla. Spread the mixture on a

Graham Crumble

4 GRAHAM CRACKERS,
   CRUMBLED

⅓ CUP BROWN SUGAR

½ TEASPOON CINNAMON

3 TABLESPOONS UNSALTED
   BUTTER

SEEDS FROM 1 VANILLA BEAN
   (OR 1 TEASPOON EXTRACT)

parchment-lined sheet tray about ½ inches thick. Roast in the oven for about 1½ hours, or until the meringues are hard.

To make the Graham Crumble: Preheat oven to 350°F. Melt the butter in the microwave. Crush graham crackers either in a bowl or food processor. In a mixing bowl, combine the graham crackers, brown sugar, cinnamon, melted butter, and vanilla. Transfer the mixture to a parchment lined sheet pan and spread evenly. Roast in the oven for 15 minutes, or until golden brown.

Assemble in individual serving bowls by placing a small scoop of the Graham Crumble on the bottom, a small amount of the chocolate mousse, and some cracked Smoked Meringue pieces over the top.

SMOKED BACON SUNDAE
SERVES 4

I'm not usually one to go over the top with a dessert, but this one is too good not to share.
Adding bacon to everything, and I do mean everything, is trendy today. Now, I love bacon as much as the
next person, but some of it is so egregious I can't bring myself to indulge, although I do commend
them for trying. Everything in moderation, right? I will admit that at first I was hesitant
about adding smoked bacon to desserts but quickly found that the salty and smokiness
from the cured pork complemented the sweetness pleasantly.

SMOKED BACON

½ CUP GRANULATED SUGAR

1 TEASPOON CAYENNE

8 STRIPS SMOKED BACON

CHANTILLY

1 CUP HEAVY CREAM

½ TEASPOON VANILLA EXTRACT

1 TABLESPOON SMOKED AGAVE
   SYRUP (PAGE 66)

BROWN BUTTER ICE CREAM
   (PAGE 170)

CANDIED NUTS AND CARAMEL
   (OPTIONAL)

Preheat the oven to 350°F.

Mix together the sugar and cayenne pepper, and use to coat the bacon.
Add as much as will stick. Place the bacon in a flat even layer on a
parchment-lined sheet tray and roast in the oven for 8 minutes. Rotate
the tray in the oven, and roast for an additional 7 minutes. Times will
vary depending on your oven. Once nicely caramelized, carefully
remove the bacon from the sheet tray and place on a cold surface.

To make the Chantilly: Whisk the cream until it forms soft peaks. Add
the vanilla and Smoked Agave Syrup, and continue whisking until still
peaks are formed. Be careful not to overwhip.

To assemble, place two scoops of Brown Butter Ice Cream in a serving
bowl, along with a large dollop of Chantilly and two pieces of Smoked
Bacon. Garnish with candied nuts and caramel, if desired.

SMOKED CHOCOLATE BROWNIE

MAKES 10 BROWNIES

In recent years, infusing smoke in common dishes has moved toward the sweet side of the culinary world. When done correctly and in moderation, applying smoke to our favorite desserts is an ingenious way of introducing new flavors to our palate. In developing this recipe, I tried smoking the different components of the brownies separately, such as the chocolate, sugar, and even the flour. While all turned out delicious, the cleanest flavor, and quite frankly, the most delicious, was when I made the brownies and then smoked the entire dessert.

---

12 OUNCES SEMISWEET
   CHOCOLATE CHIPS, DIVIDED
4 OUNCES UNSALTED BUTTER
1½ CUPS ALL-PURPOSE FLOUR
SEEDS FROM 1 VANILLA BEAN
1 CUP SMOKED SUGAR
   (PAGE 174)
½ TEASPOON BAKING SODA
2 LARGE EGGS
½ CUP ROASTED WALNUTS

Preheat both the oven and an outdoor smoker to 350°F (page 12).

In a saucepan over medium heat, add 6 ounces of the chocolate chips along with the butter and melt until homogenous. Remove from the heat and let sit for 5 minutes. Stir in the flour, sugar, vanilla, Smoked Sugar, and baking soda. Mix well. Add the eggs and mix again. Stir in the walnuts and remaining chocolate chips. Scrape the mixture onto a 9 × 9–inch or 8 × 12–inch greased baking pan and roast in the oven for 20 minutes.

Remove the pan from the oven and transfer the pan into the smoker for 12 minutes. Remove from the smoker and allow to cool before cutting and serving.

SMOKED ICE CREAM
MAKES 1 QUART

I know smoking ice cream may sound crazy to some, but it's actually not. When my restaurant first purchased an expensive Combi Oven, I was smoking everything under the sun.
The Alto-Sham CTP7, one of the more popular models in the industry, holds eight full-sized sheet trays, with one of the features being a controlled temperature smoke. You can imagine my excitement; I was like a little kid playing with his new favorite toy on Christmas morning.
But what happens when you run out of ideas with your new toy? When you have raided every corner of the savory walk-in and dry pantry? Do you abandon the adventure? Or do you go in search of new one? I hit the freezer and grabbed some ice cream. *Is it possible?* I thought *Can I smoke ice cream?*
After several attempts, it worked! Ice cream successfully smoked, and smoked well.
Smoking ice cream over alder chips added such a unique level of flavor that I had to include this exciting recipe. You can use any ice cream, but for this purpose,
I will use our Brown Butter Ice Cream (page 170).

Preheat an outdoor smoker to 350°F (page 12).

You will need two bowls or trays, the same size as each other. They must also be able to fit inside your smoker.

Fill one bowl or tray with ice. In the other, place as much ice cream as you would like to smoke. Next, place the ice cream bowl or tray on top of the ice bowl or tray. Once the smoker is at full smoke, quickly open the door and place the bowls or trays inside. Smoke hard for 5 minutes. Quickly remove from the smoker and place the ice cream immediately back into the freezer to refreeze.

ABOUT THE AUTHORS

EXECUTIVE CHEF DEREK BUGGE

Executive Chef Derek Bugge, a Cordon Bleu graduate, has worked the grill at notable taquerias, bars, restaurants, oyster houses, champagne parlors, and country clubs throughout the Pacific Northwest. He draws inspiration from his Latin roots. Time spent in the kitchen with parents and family has taught the veteran chef how properly burning, charring, and smoking ordinary foods increases the flavor profile of many dishes while entertaining friends and guests with new menu options that draws them in and whets their appetite. Today, Chef Bugge is a chef at Ascend Prime Steak & Sushi, soon to be one of the hottest new restaurants in Bellevue, Washington.

JAMES O. FRAIOLI

Culinary author James O. Fraioli has twenty-eight celebrated cookbooks and a James Beard Award to his credit. His titles have been featured on the Food Network, on *The Ellen DeGeneres Show*, in *O, The Oprah Magazine*, and in the *New York Times*. The author is notorious for teaming up with both celebrity and up-and-coming chefs along with world-renowned restaurants to showcase the best the culinary world has to offer. He resides in the greater Seattle area. Visit him online at www.culinarybookcreations.com.

ACKNOWLEDGMENTS

The authors would like to personally thank:

Photographer Mary Dee Mateo

Nicole Frail and the editorial team at Skyhorse Publishing

Agent Sharlene Martin & Martin Literary Management

Chef Derek Bugge would like to personally thank:

My family, especially my wife, Katie, who has supported me through thick and thin, even back when I could barely afford to keep the lights on.

Thank you to my mother, Emelia, who has shown me how to love, how to live, and most importantly, for our purposes, how to cook; to my father, John, who has taught me so much about life, including how to be a father and a husband; and to my sister, Sarah, my best friend, who has taught me how to be an outstanding person.

INDEX

CONVERSION CHARTS

METRIC AND IMPERIAL CONVERSIONS
(These conversions are rounded for convenience)

Ingredient	Cups/Tablespoons/Teaspoons	Ounces	Grams/Milliliters
Butter	1 cup = 16 tablespoons = 2 sticks	8 ounces	230 grams
Cheese, shredded	1 cup	4 ounces	110 grams
Cream cheese	1 tablespoon	0.5 ounce	14.5 grams
Cornstarch	1 tablespoon	0.3 ounce	8 grams
Flour, all-purpose	1 cup/1 tablespoon	4.5 ounces/0.3 ounce	125 grams/8 grams
Flour, whole wheat	1 cup	4 ounces	120 grams
Fruit, dried	1 cup	4 ounces	120 grams
Fruits or veggies, chopped	1 cup	5 to 7 ounces	145 to 200 grams
Fruits or veggies, pureed	1 cup	8.5 ounces	245 grams
Honey, maple syrup, or corn syrup	1 tablespoon	0.75 ounce	20 grams
Liquids: cream, milk, water, or juice	1 cup	8 fluid ounces	240 milliliters
Oats	1 cup	5.5 ounces	150 grams
Salt	1 teaspoon	0.2 ounce	6 grams
Spices: cinnamon, cloves, ginger, or nutmeg (ground)	1 teaspoon	0.2 ounce	5 milliliters
Sugar, brown, firmly packed	1 cup	7 ounces	200 grams
Sugar, white	1 cup/1 tablespoon	7 ounces/0.5 ounce	200 grams/12.5 grams
Vanilla extract	1 teaspoon	0.2 ounce	4 grams

OVEN TEMPERATURES

Fahrenheit	Celsius	Gas Mark
225°	110°	¼
250°	120°	½
275°	140°	1
300°	150°	2
325°	160°	3
350°	180°	4
375°	190°	5
400°	200°	6
425°	220°	7
450°	230°	8